Sent Home To Die

Sent Home To Die

DOROTHY SHELL

Pacific Press Publishing Association
Boise, Idaho
Oshawa, Ontario, Canada

Edited by Marvin Moore
Designed by Tim Larson
Cover Illustration by Robert Hunt
Type set in 10/12 Century Schoolbook

Library of Congress Catalog Card Number: 87-62293

ISBN 0-8163-0769-5

87 88 89 90 91 • 5 4 3 2 1

Acknowledgments

I wish to thank my husband, Vince, and our sons, Alan, Rick, and Dennis, without whose help this book and my recovery would have been impossible. They believed in me and held me up when giving up would have been so much easier.

My thanks goes also to those whom God placed in my life to help in putting this book together: Laura Smothers, Ginger Blackburn, Marilyn Donahue, and the many others who spent hours typing and critiquing. Without them I could not have completed this great task.

Mostly, I thank a loving heavenly Father whose presence makes life bearable and whose still small voice finally convinced me that if I would quit asking for help and take pen in hand, He would give me the words and energy to complete what He placed in my heart. I must tell others that no matter what the circumstances, God is always there, giving us the courage and ability to withstand anything the world has to offer.

Dorothy Shell

Contents

Preface		9
Medical Diagnosis		11
Chapter 1:	Beginnings	13
Chapter 2:	Living With Pain	21
Chapter 3:	Crisis	25
Chapter 4:	The Answer	29
Chapter 5:	The Decision	33
Chapter 6:	Dark Days	39
Chapter 7:	Telling the Boys	43
Chapter 8:	The Promise	47
Chapter 9:	The Elks	53
Chapter 10:	Sent Home to Die	59
Chapter 11:	Home Again	63
Chapter 12:	Ministering Saints	69
Chapter 13:	Beginning to Live Again	75
Chapter 14:	Job's Comforters	81
Chapter 15:	Help Is in Sight	85
Chapter 16:	Looking Back	91

Preface

My heart's desire is that my struggle to find faith for the healing of my body may inspire those who are undergoing similar trials. God does care, and He actually suffers with us when His answer must be "No," or, "Wait a while." This is a truth I want to share. God does not always heal all our diseases in this life, but He does go with us through the pain and sorrow. Psalm 139:13 tells me that God "made all the delicate, inner parts of my body, and knit them together in my mother's womb." LB. Since I was born with the affliction that has haunted me every day of my life, I believe that God knit me thus. I do not say that He willed that I should suffer thus, except in the sense that He allowed the defect in me that an imperfect heredity bestowed. In His infinite wisdom, He deemed me strong enough to trust me with this strange malady that others might be blessed.

I know that He has been with me and has given me many new and useful experiences each time I walked through the dark valley; I can share in the suffering of others because of my own walk through the valley of the shadow of death. I believe that each period of pain and suffering had a purpose.

While undergoing an extremely severe time of suffering, I one day cried out to God, "Why, Lord, why? Either heal me or give me some hope of being able to use this for your glory." I decided to search the Scriptures. I opened to 2 Corinthians 12:7-10. These words seemed to leap out at me:

"I will say this: because these experiences I had were so tremendous, God was afraid I might be puffed up by them; so I was given a physical condition which has been a thorn in my flesh, a messenger from Satan to hurt and bother me, and prick my pride. Three different times I begged God to make me well again. Each time he said, 'No. But I am with you; that is all you need. My power shows up best in weak people.' Now I am glad to boast about how weak I am; I am glad to be a living demonstration of Christ's power, instead of showing off my own power and abilities. Since I know it is all for Christ's good, I am quite happy about 'the thorn,' and about insults and hardships, persecutions and difficulties; for when I am weak, then I am strong—the less I have, the more I depend on him."

I believe God spoke these words to me that day, and I have had peace in my soul ever since.

I believe God works with each of us individually to reach a lost world. I am willing to carry my share of the load.

"Be still, and know that I am God." Psalm 46:10 helps me wait and lean on Him for comfort and strength in the times of trial.

——Dorothy Shell

Medical Diagnosis

The following diagnosis of Dorothy Shell's disease was written by her family physician, Bernard P. Strouth, M.D.:

Dorothy Shell was admitted to St. Alphonsus Hospital [in Boise, Idaho] in 1964, with a flulike illness. She was also nervous, depressed, and suffering from a myriad of aches and pains which were not compatible with any apparent physical illness. During the course of her hospitalization, several events occurred, some by accident, and some in therapeutic attempts which resulted in diagnosing the classic symptom complex of acute intermittent porphyria. The triggering mechanism in this patient was probably the use of Seconal for sleep—a proper hypnotic in those days for people with insomnia. This, however, triggered a neuritis so severe that the patient's respiratory muscles became paralyzed—a complication which resulted in pneumonia, and which subsequently resulted in the need for a tracheotomy to help the patient get rid of the pooled pulmonary secretions. Quite by accident, the urine which was part of the routine examination was left exposed in the lab for a couple of hours and turned black. The entire disease process became evident, and the diagnosis of acute porphyria was made. It was subsequently verified here and at the University of Washington in Seattle and by other labs, including those of Dr. C. J. Watson at Northwestern Hospital in Minneapolis. Dr. Watson, historically, was perhaps the first physician to recognize the disease as an entity.

Acute intermittent porphyria is a disease transmitted as a hereditary dominant character which results in increased porphyrin formation and characterized clinically by abdominal pain, peripheral neuritis and, commonly, nervous disorders. Porphyrins are a part of the body's energy storage component and also are part of the synthesis of hemoglobin. Defects in the enzymes which contribute to the degradation of porphyrins and to their overproduction are metabolically the cause of the disorder. The major treatment of porphyria consists in abstinence from many medications—a fact which is extremely difficult for porphyria victims to accept or understand. So, much treatment time is spent reiterating a single message—Don't take X, Y, and Z because it will indeed make you feel worse instead of better. Some new treatments are emerging, however, including hemin infusions which have been shown to be effective in at least some of the patients.

Porphyria is likely to be cured one day when appropriate preventative procedures and further knowledge of the disease is available. We may at this time be on the horizon of this breakthrough.

Chapter 1
Beginnings

That day began just like a thousand others. I awoke with a terrible pain in my sides. This pain had become my constant companion for as long as I could remember, except now each time it was more severe.

"Mom," I called. "I just can't go to school today. My sides are hurting really bad, and I feel sick to my stomach."

It was my junior year in high school. We lived on a farm near Caldwell, Idaho, at the time. Mom knew I wouldn't miss school unless I was very ill, so she permitted me to stay in bed. I often had such days, but this time, as the morning progressed, so did the pain.

Each time the pain began, it seemed to start in my lower abdomen with a constant ache and gradually progress to a sharp, piercing pain, like knives tearing away at my insides. The waves of pain soon moved to my lower back, even encompassing my legs. My body involuntarily curled into a ball. It seemed as if by curling up I could somehow alleviate some of the pain. No relief came. Instead, the pain increased, and eventually I became delirious. Mom was frightened. She called Dad, and they rushed me to the doctor.

"Mrs. Goertzen," the doctor said, "these side aches have become so severe and are occurring with such frequency that I feel Dorothy may be suffering from appendicitis. I think we need to perform an operation, and I think we had best do it now."

After the surgery the doctor called Mom and Dad into his office. "We are at a loss to understand Dorothy's problem," he said. "The problem is not the appendix. I did, however, find a few other problems that could have caused some of the pain, but not to the extent that she is having. I simply cannot explain it." The doctor shook his head. His inability to pinpoint the problem obviously disturbed him a great deal.

Dad and Mom were worried as they left the doctor's office. "What can we do for Dorothy?" Mom asked. "Surely someone, somewhere, can find out what is wrong."

"She'll probably outgrow it," was all Dad said.

I returned home after eleven days of unexplainable agony. Slowly I began to recuperate and resume my studies. Then one night I woke up and the pain was back, piercing my sides.

"A bad dream. Yes, I'm having a bad dream," I thought. The shadows on the walls were like tormentors hovering over me, taunting me. "I must wake up!"

Stabbing pain shot through me. Every part of my body responded in jerks and tremors. I realized that I was not asleep. Even a dream could not be this bad. "Not again. Oh Lord, help me, not this again," I cried.

My crying awoke my sister, Vi, whose bed I shared. Even in the darkened room she could tell something was terribly wrong.

"What's wrong, Dorothy? Are you hurting again? Hold on. I'll run and get Mom."

Mom hurried into our room. One look told her that the problem had not been solved by the recent surgery. She held me close, wrapped me in one of her homemade quilts, and waited for the pain to subside. When it persisted they rushed me to the hospital again. The pain was so severe that I felt I had to tear on something the way the pain was tearing at my insides. On the way to the hospital I actually began tearing the quilt Mom had wrapped me in. I felt completely out of control.

By the time we arrived at the hospital, I had lost all feeling in my legs and arms. I did not know it, but I was very close to death. I was rushed into the emergency room, where doctors and nurses worked wildly to keep me alive. When my condition stabilized, I was taken to a room and kept for tests and observation.

Again the doctors could not discover any physical reason for the pain and the loss of feeling in my legs and arms. They couldn't explain why I had nearly died in the emergency room. They finally decided that the ordeal must be just nerves. So they reasoned, and so they explained to my parents. "We are baffled by your daughter's pain and loss of feeling in her limbs," they said. "Could she possibly be needing more attention than you are giving her?"

I don't know what Mom told the doctors. I'm sure it never occurred to her that she could give more attention to one of her ten children than to another. "You just treat them all alike," she so often remarked.

"Sometimes girls can fake symptoms if they feel they aren't given enough attention," the doctor said. "Could this be her problem?"

Dad and Mom could not accept this explanation. They knew that I was a happy, outgoing person when I was feeling well. Mom was gravely disturbed. She knew there had to be a reason for the pain, the frequent nausea, and the other symptoms I was having. Something was terribly wrong, but to whom could she turn?

As the days passed, again I seemingly bounced back from this experience to the energetic person I was between those dreadful attacks. I felt well for a time and was soon back in school and my first love, sports. I loved to play basketball. When my health permitted, basketball demanded all the time my folks would allow me to spend on it.

My senior year in high school was an exciting one. My parents had moved again, and wanting to finish my last year at Notus High School, near Caldwell, Idaho, I began riding to school with a teacher from our area. Basketball's being high on my priority list made getting to and from games somewhat of a problem. I often stayed at school and rode to basketball games on the school bus. One night after the game, I realized that I would not have a way to get home.

"Maybe we can take you home," Coleen, a friend of mine suggested. "Don and I are riding with another guy who has a car. His name is Vince Shell. He's a really nice guy, and I think he'll be glad to see that you get home. I'll ask him."

I did not know that this "guy," Vince, had been watching me for some time and had been waiting for an opportunity to meet me. I was just glad for the ride. As we walked out of the gymnasium into the frosty January night air, Vince slipped his arm around me, ostensibly to help me across the icy, snow-covered ground.

"So, you're my date tonight," he said.

I tried to step away from the circle of his arm. "Not really a date, Mr. Shell," I said. I started to pull away, but my foot slipped on a spot of ice and I fell flat, pulling him down with me. Just then someone in a waiting bus turned on the lights, and everyone laughed and cheered. Vince picked himself up, helped me to my feet, grinned sheepishly, and quipped, "Boy, you sure fell for me."

Although I didn't realize it then, I guess I did. It didn't take me long to realize that Vince was no ordinary guy and that my interest in him was not going to be a passing fancy. As the days went by, I began thinking about Vince most of the time. We spent long, happy winter evenings together. Our mutual belief and trust in God drew us closer.

Vince attended church with me for a time, but soon I was going with him to his church, a small white church in a village called Middleton. It had the appearance of a country church. Everyone seemed like family. They loved, nurtured, and helped us grow in the admonition of God. It was in this small church that we were married on a beautiful August day in 1950—a treasured day for a treasured experience.

Within a short time Vince was to learn the meaning of the words he said, "For better or for worse, in sickness and in health."

There could not have been a happier couple than Mr. and Mrs. Vincent Shell as we left on our honeymoon trip to McCall, Idaho, a beautiful mountain resort town nestled in the pines beside a magnificent mountain lake. I could scarcely contain the absolute bliss I felt. I snuggled up close to my handsome young husband.

We arrived late in the evening and rented a room in the town

hotel. Vince signed the register "Mr. and Mrs. Vincent Shell."
My face flushed. I was sure the hotel clerk knew we were just
married just by looking at us.

The setting was beautiful, a perfect place for a honeymoon.
The days were warm and exciting as we spent time boating,
swimming, and just walking hand in hand along the beaches.

Our first home together was very small. It didn't even have
bathroom facilities, but to us it was a little piece of heaven. For
me, it was the culmination of all my dreams. Here I was, clean-
ing, cooking, and washing for the man I loved. I was determined
to be a good wife. Vince made me feel that everything I did was
just that.

Then it happened again. Only this time I was more
nauseated than ever. I awoke one morning feeling very sick. I
tried to keep it from Vince, but by the time he came home in
the evening I could hide it no longer. "Oh, Honey," I cried, "do
you remember about the awful sickness I told you about? Well,
I'm afraid it's back. I'm so sick I can hardly stand."

Vince quickly found a doctor and took me to see him. After
examining me, he told me that I was pregnant. The illness from
which I suffered had intensified the usual nausea. Any medication the doctor prescribed only made me sicker. As before, the
doctor could not understand what the problem might be. Now
with a baby on the way and the pain and nausea intensified, I
was really frightened.

The nausea and pain became my constant companions. Some
days I felt I couldn't make myself move. I wanted to roll up in
a little ball and shut out everyone and everything, but my desire
to please Vince was greater than my suffering. I refused to surrender to this terrible thing that haunted me day and night.
Some days it seemed virtually impossible to keep going, but
with God's help and Vince's understanding, I managed.

The months passed quickly. Alan, our first son, was born on
May 26, 1951. He was the light of our life, such a beautiful
result of our love for each other.

I continued to have severe bouts of pain. We sought help
from numerous doctors. No one seemed to understand what the
problem was, often telling Vince that it was just nerves and

not to take it too seriously. I'm sure that many times he felt exasperated, wondering how to cope with all that was going on. I, too, felt the frustration. It seemed as though I was constantly asking, "Why, Lord? Why can't I get over this? What have I done to deserve this? Help me, Lord. Help me make it through this day."

Then came times of calm and little pain. These days seemed so good, and I would pray for it to last. Each time I felt sure it would not happen again.

It wasn't long till Rick, our second son, arrived on the scene. Rick was born on our second anniversary. What a wonderful anniversary gift! Again our hearts were full of love for this, another son.

Our third son, Dennis, came on July 27, two years later, to complete our family. I was content. Three wonderful sons and a husband who adored me. What more could I want from life? Now if only I could be rid of the pain that controlled so much of my time. *If only.*

On one of my numerous visits to the doctor, he told me that he would like to do exploratory surgery. He felt that there could be something other than nerves causing such pain. During the surgery he performed a complete hysterectomy. "I'm sure we have found the answer to Dorothy's problem," he assured Vince as he came out of the operating room.

Instead, the pain immediately intensified—even before I left the hospital. The more drugs I received, the worse I became. My heels became raw from jerking them back and forth on the stiff hospital sheets. My elbows ached from the constant turning, trying to find relief. The pain tore through my body till I cried out for help, first to the doctor, and then frantically to God. I felt as if God had turned a deaf ear. "Why, Lord?" I cried. "Why? Where are You?"

"Vince," Doctor Dedman said one evening as he visited me in the hospital, "I think we should try psychotherapy. Dorothy can't go on like this, and I don't know of any physical cause for such pain."

They asked me how I felt about psychiatric treatment. "I'll try anything," I sobbed wildly. "Just help me."

Since it was a weekend and they would not start the treatment until Monday, I wanted desperately to go home and see the boys first. I pleaded, "Please, let me go home for just these two days."

The doctor and Vince tried to persuade me to stay in the hospital, but my determination won out. When I reached home and the medication I had been given was stopped, I began to improve. No one connected the added severity of the attacks to the drugs they had given me. When I began to feel better, I persuaded Vince to allow me to stay home a little longer. As I continued to improve, I determined not to return to that hospital. The fear of another attack brought on by anything they might give me frightened me. I never went back for the treatment.

As the attacks of pain subsided, I began to enjoy my family again. A loving heavenly Father knew what was in store for me and had given me a family to love and cherish. He understood that I would need a reason for living in the dark days ahead.

Chapter 2
Living With Pain

As my strength returned, I determined to enjoy my family to the fullest. Nothing would keep me from making a happy home for them. Perhaps my own childhood, which had been scarce on playtime, influenced my decision to give my children time for playing and daydreaming.

Our favorite pastime was camping. At first we didn't have a tent, so we slept out under the stars, taking the children into our sleeping bags to keep them warm. We cooked over a crackling campfire. The excitement of doing things with the family helped me cope with the ever-recurring pain. Vince and the boys still look forward to spending time together camping out in the beautiful mountains of Idaho.

As the boys grew older, our interests included school as well as church activities. Vince and I were involved in the local PTA, even becoming presidents. At our church we were appointed youth directors and took the boys with us to youth camps and outings. We taught youth classes, attended church picnics, camp meetings, and any other activity that involved the family. For me, any day without pain or debilitating fatigue was a day of praise. On those days, I tried to make up for all the times when I simply could not do the extra things I longed to do.

At times Vince would ask, "Honey, don't you think we should cut out some of these activities? You're pushing yourself too hard, aren't you?"

"The only way I can keep above this thing is to keep busy," I would answer emphatically.

The thing that made it so difficult for others to understand was the fact that I did not look ill. I could be hurting terribly, and some dear person in church would invariably say, "My, you look well today, Dorothy. I'm glad you're feeling OK."

"If you only knew," I would think, but I would try to smile and reply, "Thanks, I'm fine." I felt that no one understood enough to share my burden. What a lonely thing pain is—a very personal thing that others cannot understand unless they've been there too. Instead of understanding, I often received rejection.

I should have been learning that the Lord understands and upholds us in such times, but I was often too busy doing *for* Him to take time to communicate *with* Him. I would learn this lesson in due time, but in the meantime I continued to question, "Why is this happening to me? Where is God when I hurt so bad?"

When I refused to go back to the hospital after my hysterectomy, the doctor suggested to Vince that perhaps I was seeking sympathy and he should just ignore my "attacks" of illness. "Try not to be so sympathetic, and the pain may disappear."

Vince tried to follow the doctor's advice. I understood how he felt, but I could not control the pain. Again I cried out to God, "What is going to happen to me? To us? To our marriage?" Each time I returned to the doctor I pleaded for help, but even if he believed me, he didn't seem to know what to do.

Added to the physical suffering was the mental torture, as I thought about what this was doing to our family. The day would begin fairly well with my determination to be in control. I wanted to greet Vince with a smile and a hug when he came home at night, but by evening I invariably found myself yelling at the boys and meeting Vince with tears streaming down my cheeks.

Many nights after Vince was sleeping, I lay awake thinking back over the day. I felt like my heart would break. Hot tears streamed down my cheeks and fell silently on my pillow. "Where are You, God. Can't You hear me? Don't You care?" The quietness was unbroken. No answer came. I waited, impatiently and sometimes angrily, but no release came.

I measured my Christian experience by God's willingness to take away my illness. When it seemed that He did not hear me, I felt rejected. I began to believe that I must have done something very sinful, and that was why God refused to heal me. Yet there were days when I could sense Him there upholding me, even though the pain did not go away.

Many times during the long, sleepless nights, as I yielded to my fears, my crying would awaken Vince.

"Having trouble sleeping, Honey?" he would ask as he held me close. "What can I do? We've tried everything. I just don't know what to do anymore. Tell me what I can do."

"Please hold me close; just hold me close. That helps more than anything."

Sometimes we'd both cry for a while in frustration. Eventually, we would both drop off to a restless sleep.

Mornings, when Vince had gone to work and the boys to school, I wondered, "How much longer can Vince handle all this crying without giving up on me?" I worked desperately to control my response to pain, and with Vince's love, and I'm sure God's sustaining grace, I managed to handle much of it. By trial and error, I learned various ways to cope during the hardest days. When I felt the pain coming on, I made plans to do something special. Quickly doing household chores, I would have coffee with a neighbor or go shopping or take drives. If I kept busy enough, the days often passed and I would still be in control. This did not always work, but trying made it easier.

These were difficult years for Vince. He loved me—there was no doubt about that. He longed to help and tried to understand. Many husbands would have given up and left, but he remained loving even though he did not understand.

The years hastened by. We celebrated our thirteenth anniversary. I was grateful for all the good times we shared, but as the attacks became more frequent, the fatigue and nervousness became more intense. The days that lay ahead were to be a test of faith and endurance. Only God would know the outcome.

Chapter 3
Crisis

I opened the kitchen door and stepped outside. What a beautiful morning! After a long winter, it seemed so good to see the spring flowers blooming. "Vince, come look. There's a crocus coming up," I cried.

He joined me, slipping an arm around me. "Where's my breakfast?" he teased, as he smiled and pulled me closer.

How good the warm weather seemed after the long, cold winter! How eagerly I had looked forward to the summer months, hoping I would feel better this year. This morning, however, I had no thought except the joy of the gentle breeze blowing softly across my face and the new life springing up all around me.

"Look, there's a daffodil! I feel like this is going to be a special day!"

Vince shared my enthusiasm. He smiled fondly and said, "We'll soon be able to go camping, Honey, and yup, this does feel like a special day." As he turned he added, "Now come and get my breakfast. I've got to get to work."

I watched as a lazy white cloud drifted by, and thought, "Thank You, God, for such a lovely day—for love and life, and, yes, for spring."

As I returned to my kitchen I felt an unexpected happiness in the chores that claimed my immediate attention.

The boys scrambled to the table. As usual, they were hungry and in a hurry to get to school. The kitchen was filled with their good-natured bickering and teasing. Vince quickly ordered attention. "Let's have a little quiet around here," he said as he smiled fondly at the three sons he adored.

The boys were all towheads, but that's where the resemblance ended. Each was developing his own personality. Alan and Rick were so close in age they were like twins, but they were opposites, nevertheless. Alan, the most sensitive, was twelve years old. He was becoming a real student. Rick, a year younger, was a born leader. He took life in stride and was generous to a fault. Denny, nine, was a good deal smaller than his brothers. He didn't let it bother him, though. "I can lick you both!" he would boast. I heard it a thousand times.

Suddenly, as I began to place breakfast on the table, a terrible wave of nausea swept over me, leaving me breathless. I reached for the edge of the sink and held on tightly. "Oh, no. Not again. Please not today."

I struggled for control. My mind whirled, and a thick black cloud seemed to settle over me. I gripped the sink harder and shook my head back and forth, trying to brush away the feeling. I was not going to give in to this.

Glancing up at me, Vince asked sharply, "Is anything the matter? Are you all right?"

I shook my head and answered, "It's just a queasy feeling, I guess. I'm all right."

I regained my composure and was able to get Vince and the boys off to work and school. But I *wasn't* all right. The nausea persisted, and as the day progressed, so did the old, familiar pain. It swept over me again and again, like a never-ending tide. A heavy cloud closed around me. I tried lying down, but it would not go away.

By the time Vince came home from work, I was too sick to hold up my head. He had seen me go through rough times before, but I could tell by the expression on his face that he knew this was different. Vince called Dr. Strouth, who prescribed medicine for the flu that was making its rounds in the community. I swallowed the pills obediently. As usual I became worse. Dr. Strouth prescribed other drugs. I took them too. Soon my nerves began reacting to the medication until I could no longer control them. I wanted to lash out at those who were doing their best to help me. Every nerve screamed for help, a warning that no one seemed to understand.

The doctor told Vince that he thought I might be having a nervous breakdown. I was frantic. I tried pulling myself together, but the terrible pain and the mental anguish became too much to endure.

I was vaguely aware that the boys were standing by my bed crying as they watched me lose control. I could hear my own voice like a desperate, unfinished prayer, "My God, my God, why have You forsaken me?" Somehow I knew He loved me, but why was He allowing this to happen?

I felt like I was exploding and the shattered pieces of my conscious mind were being hurled in a million directions. "Oh, help me!" I cried, "Won't somebody help me!" The words formed in my throat, struggled to get out, then died away and became no more than trapped thoughts, caught up in darkness and despair.

Frightened and confused, Vince called the doctor again. "Doctor, please meet me at the hospital; I'm taking Dorothy in. She can't go on like this. You *must* do something." His voice reflected the urgency of the problem.

By the time we arrived at the hospital I had lost all sense of reality. I was whisked into a private room where the doctor was waiting, ready to administer a glucose intravenous. Vince was told to go home to the boys and get some rest. They would research the problem more in the morning.

I was oblivious of the trip to the hospital. I was only aware of the terrible agony, and then came darkness. Like a warm blanket, unconsciousness wrapped around me and brought relief. When consciousness returned, so did the pain. Fear tore through me with a force as shattering as the pain. I wanted to run away, to crawl from the bed, to leave my body. My head tossed back and forth on the pillow, trying to deny what I knew was true: There was no escape.

I became aware of a nurse standing over me. "Mrs. Shell, Mrs. Shell, can you hear me? Mrs. Shell, we're going to take some tests to see if we can find out what's going on here."

She ushered me into a little room and helped me onto a table next to a strange-looking machine. I was hardly settled before she began strapping me down.

"What are you doing?" I screamed. I was frantic.

"Standard procedure," came her tart reply.

It was torture. Screams rose in my throat, but I refused to allow them to come out. I was trembling all over. No one explained what was happening. Unfamiliar doctors came into the room and watched intently as dye traveled through my body.

"Oh, God, why are You letting this happen to me?"

As if in answer to my prayer, darkness came once again, bringing blessed oblivion.

When I opened my eyes, Vince was with me. I braced myself for the pain, but it didn't come. The drugs given for the flu had worn off, I was more calm, and my mind seemed to be working again. Vince reached across the white sheet and took my hand, cradling it in his hand. I could see the lines of weariness and worry. I knew this sickness was taking its toll on my husband and my family.

"I feel so much better. Let's ask the doctor if I can go home," I begged.

Vince gave me a reassuring hug as he answered, "I want you to stay until the doctor says everything is all right."

Any hopes I had for returning home that day were dashed when Vince met with Dr. Strouth later in the day.

"Vince," the doctor began, "I really think we should place Dorothy in the psychiatric ward for some tests. It seems to me this illness could be mental. We call it psychosomatic. We've searched every avenue and can find no cause for the way she is acting. This seems to be our only alternative."

Vince assured the doctor that if there was anything they could do to find the source of my illness, we were for it.

Vince returned to my room. Gently he touched my face. He hesitated before he told me what the doctor had said. I could not argue. It didn't matter anymore. The only thing that mattered was that someone would help me. With our approval I was moved to the psychiatric ward where the "tests" were to begin.

Chapter 4
The Answer

As far as the hospital was concerned, I was a mental patient now, and the "tests" the doctor ordered were a series of shock treatments. I recall very little about them, except that I was taken into a small room where I was placed on a narrow table, and I was terribly frightened.

The nurses busied themselves by hooking an apparatus to my head. Unanswered questions raced through my mind. "Will this hurt? Will it help me? Vince, where are you?"

A doctor entered the room and nodded to one of the nurses. She moved toward me. I closed my eyes. When darkness came this time there was nothing—no remembrances, no dreams, just a deep void suspended in time. I remember nothing else until I woke up in my room.

After the second treatment, I discovered on awakening that I was having difficulty moving my arms and legs.

"My arm!" I cried, "Why can't I move my arm?" No one answered. No one came. Nobody paid any attention at all. Again and again I tried to raise it. It was like dead weight and remained strangely lifeless. I lay quietly, determined to quell the fear within me. Periodically I tried again, and again. My arm lay motionless as if it were not a part of me. I cried with relief when the feeling gradually began to return.

However, when I awoke the next morning my arm was still useless. I called frantically for the nurse, but no one seemed to believe me. I had forgotten: I was considered a mental patient now and could be expected to imagine anything. Terror filled me! "Am I still sleeping? Is this a nightmare?" I strained to make the muscles move. "Move, move!" I commanded. Nothing. Then I knew. "I'm not sleeping. This is not a nightmare." In fact, it was only an indication of a horrible nightmare that was just beginning, and that would be all too real.

I was relieved when a nurse finally appeared at the door. I tried to tell her what was happening, but I stopped when I saw the expression on her face. Her large size and her brisk manner intimidated me. I knew some of the nurses thought I was mentally disturbed, and I had almost begun to believe them. I looked at her pleadingly.

"Get out of bed." Her voice was harsh and impersonal. "I'm taking you in for a tub bath."

"I—I can't walk," I stammered. "My legs won't work. I keep trying to make them move, but they just won't." I could feel my face crumple as I began to cry.

"Nonsense," she snapped, "You're just being ornery. Come on, now, get out of that bed." She grabbed me and yanked me onto the floor. When my legs gave way, she became angry. "Going to be stubborn, are you? Well, we'll see who is the stubborn one around here!"

With that she linked her arms around me and literally dragged me down the hallway and bodily threw me into the tub. My head cracked against the side, and my arms and legs twisted painfully beneath me. I couldn't believe what was happening to me. I was frightened and hurting. My mind began to whirl. My thoughts spun.

"Why are these things happening to me?" I sobbed. "Lord, where are You now, when I need You? What have I done to deserve this? God, don't You hear me?" This prayer seemed to pour out like a broken record. I had never known such despair. I felt like an animal in a trap, too frightened to move and in too much pain to try.

It seemed so long ago that I had stood outside my own home and looked at the spring flowers blooming. Days passed, each one worse than the one before, with no relief from pain or depression. I longed to leave my bed and run far away—anywhere. I wanted to hide, but there was no escape. Neither could I rest, for every nerve in my body throbbed. I wanted to scream, "I haven't lost my mind. Don't you see? This is real. This is *really* happening. Oh, God, make someone believe me!"

Dr. Cornell, the doctor who had given the shock treatments, telephoned Dr. Strouth. "There's something terribly wrong here, and it's definitely not mental. I have no ideas to offer, but Dorothy has a very serious problem. If we don't find it in a hurry, she won't be here to need our help."

"Are you saying that the shock treatments aren't helping?" Dr. Strouth asked.

"Definitely. I won't put her through any more of them. She must be moved where she can receive more intensive care."

I was moved, and the frantic search began to find the problem. But the paralysis slowly spread over the rest of my body. I could move at first. The muscles just seemed reluctant to respond. But the responses grew slower and slower until one day there was no reaction at all. I was paralyzed, but I was not immune to the pain. The abdominal pain became less severe, but it stayed with me—my constant, unwanted companion.

All I could do now was lie in bed, unmoving, waiting for the results from another batch of tests. Tubes ran from my arms to intravenous bottles hanging overhead. Oh, how I longed to leave this place! How I wanted to go home to Vince, home to our children. My eyes clouded with tears. I wanted to be a wife and mother. Instead, I was a burden.

The interminable tests continued. Fear invaded my thoughts and haunted my dreams. At night, the tears would roll down my cheeks, and I yearned for the comfort of Vince's arms. If only he could hold me close again, I wouldn't be so afraid.

One day, quite by accident, the urine specimen which was part of a routine examination was left on a window ledge. When it was found, it had turned black. This triggered a remembrance of a disease that the lab technician had read about, that manifested itself in this manner. The diagnosis was made and verified.

"Porphyria," the doctor said. The word meant nothing to me. I couldn't ask questions, for by now the paralysis was spreading to my vocal chords, but I listened eagerly. A diagnosis, even one with a strange name, was what we had been waiting for.

"Dorothy," he went on, "porphyria is a rare blood disease. Few people have it, and we don't know much about it. But we do know drugs make it worse. We could have spared you so much pain if we had only known, if we had listened to you."

A glimmer of hope! They knew what the trouble was and had given it a name. I wasn't a mental case. I had not been imagining things. I closed my eyes and breathed a prayer of thankfulness. Surely, now that the doctors knew what was wrong, they would know how to cure it.

The doctor left. I had no way of knowing that he had gone to find Vince.

"Vince," the doctor said, "we think Dorothy has porphyria."

Vince's excitement was short-lived. "Even though the knowledge may help others," the doctor said, "it is probably too late for Dorothy. In such an acute stage, the disease is usually fatal. Every day she is losing control of another muscle. Today, when you visit her, she won't be able to talk to you. Her vocal chords seem to be paralyzing too."

He put his arm around Vince's shoulders. "If by some miracle Dorothy lives, she can never be much more than a vegetable. You're going to have to face the facts, and the future."

This was Vince and Dorothy Shell the doctor was talking about. It wasn't the guy next door. It was us, our family he was talking to. The world, all the world Vince cared most about, was falling apart.

Vince left the hospital that day without coming to see me. He told me later that he drove along the streets toward our church, functioning like a piece of machinery, unable to think or feel. He talked to our pastor, Bob Cantrell, then tried to go back to work. He knew he wasn't alone, but oh, how alone he felt! How could he keep his job when he needed to be with me? How could he make a life for his sons? How could he climb a mountain that was too high?

But I didn't know what was happening to Vince. I didn't know what the doctor had told him. I only lay on my hospital bed, unable to move, unable to speak. But I could breathe. I could still breathe.

Chapter 5
The Decision

At first it didn't occur to me that I might die. Paralysis had now progressed to the point that I was unable to move any muscles at all. Even when I slept, my eyelids never closed. Those who sat with me learned to tell by the expression in my eyes whether I was awake. I could do nothing for myself. At times I couldn't even breathe. A little machine, which the nurses called "the bird," had to be used when my breathing became too difficult.

Because of my inability to move, my lungs began to fill with fluid. Daily I grew weaker. There were days when breathing was extremely difficult, and fluid gurgled up and down my chest. I lay quietly. The stark white walls of my tiny room seemed to close in around me. The nurses and family who filtered in and out spoke in muted whispers. I had the frightening feeling that they were keeping something from me.

"What is it?" I wanted to cry out. "What is it I'm not supposed to know?" No words came. Only tears.

I had a sense of time passing, of minutes ticking by too quickly, as if someone had wound a clock too tightly.

I tried desperately to move. "Stop! Don't go on without me!" I could only stare at the ceiling and wait. I was going nowhere, and again I had the strange feeling that my time was running out.

My body ached from lying so still. I wanted desperately to move my arms, my legs, my head, or just have someone turn me again, but I could not convey this to anyone. The pain was

33

like an oppressive dream from which I could not awaken. As the days dragged by, my thoughts turned frequently to God, where questions went over and over in my mind like a broken record.

"If God is so loving and cares so much for us, why does He allow us to suffer so? If He wanted me to die, why didn't He just take me without all this agony?" I asked myself in bitter frustration. "God, what more could I have done? Didn't I go to church regularly? I taught in children's church. Vince and I spent hours with the youth, even giving up our vacations to help in youth camps and youth trips. Remember . . . remember . . . !"

I had believed in a religion of good works. But now I wondered: Was that enough, or did God ask for something more? I had plenty of time to lie still and think about it. Oh, how difficult the lesson of stillness was.

My mind gradually became more receptive to the Spirit of God. My heart yearned to know Him better. I was learning what it really meant to "be still, and know that I am God." Psalm 46:10. I was still, not because I wanted to be, but because He had allowed me to be, that I might learn to know Him better.

Before all this, when I felt well enough, I was always on the move, day and night. There was so much to do, there were so many places to go, so many people to see. I had always relished quiet moments with my children and Vince, but I had seldom taken time to be still in order to know God. My conversations with Him were hurried snatches, delivered on the run:

"Lord, thank You for helping me."

"Dear Father, please help me with the boys."

And as always, "Please, please, take away this pain."

After a busy day, there were times when I began a prayer, but would fall asleep before I could finish. I would promise myself and God that tomorrow I would do better. But tomorrow never seemed to come—until now. Lying motionless in my hospital bed, there was no more rushing or hurrying or pushing God into the background.

I began to listen. The hospital was full of sounds: Voices in the corridors, the metallic rattle of dinner trays, the soft whirring sounds of wheels against the polished floors, the bustle and rush of the daytime schedule and the softer whispers of night. Life was going on all around me. I heard its steady rhythm and felt its pulse. But I lay separated from the hum, isolated and alive, but not really among the living.

With nothing but time on my hands, I blocked out the hospital sounds and began to listen for God's "still, small voice." Pleading my good works had only brought frustration, self-pity, and anger. I began to realize my deep need of God.

Lying in nearly the same position every day made my body ache. Discouragement had now become a frequent visitor in my room. It sat at my bedside and talked with me, reminding me of my desperate condition. It came in and out of my room in various ways. Sometimes it came on the nurse's tray, where waiting for me was the liquid I wanted so desperately to drink, yet could not swallow. It would even cajole me into thinking that it would be better for me and everyone else if I just gave up. Discouragement was an intruder, but with the help of the Lord, I determined not to let him in my heart.

Lying so still, my lungs began to fill even faster. My condition continued to deteriorate. Daily I grew weaker. On one of Vince's daily visits Dr. Strouth stopped him in the hallway and said, "Vince, I must talk to you in the conference room, please."

From the gravity of the doctor's voice, Vince knew that the news was not going to be good.

"Vince, Dorothy has developed a very severe case of pneumonia. Due to her paralysis, she can no longer cough up the phlegm that gathers in her lungs. She will drown in her own fluids unless a tracheotomy is performed."

"What are you waiting for?" Vince almost shouted.

"It isn't that simple. If it were, we wouldn't have hesitated this long. You see, even though it is a simple procedure, Dorothy may be too weak to even survive the surgery."

The doctor continued sympathetically. "It's a difficult decision. If we do not do the tracheotomy, she will just slip away. She is very near death anyway, and that may be the best way. However, it must be your decision."

Vince slumped into the chair, bewildered. He placed his hands over his ears, as if to close out the doctor's voice. It was a terrible decision to have thrust upon him. He had become exhausted from the heartbreaking weeks of waiting, working, and caring for the boys, and now his mind refused to bear any more.

"Doctor, I can't make a decision like that. I just can't," Vince exclaimed, holding back the tears.

Placing an arm around Vince's shoulder, Dr. Strouth said, "I've asked Dr. Patterson, a throat specialist, to examine Dorothy. If you want to wait until we have consulted with him, we will do that."

Vince felt as if he had been given a reprieve from a death sentence.

After the examination, Dr. Patterson and Dr. Strouth returned to the waiting room where Vince and the family members waited for the verdict. Pastor Bob had joined them.

"I cannot give you any hope that Dorothy will survive the operation," Dr. Patterson said. "It's obvious that she is alert by the expression in her eyes. I feel we must try to make her more comfortable by helping her to breathe more freely. Do you agree, Mr. Shell?"

"Of course. Anything, to help her. We would like to spend a few minutes alone with her first, doctor."

As the family and Pastor Bob gathered around my bed, fear was evident on their faces. I wanted to put my arms around Vince and tell him how much I loved him and our sons, how much I appreciated his love and understanding. I prayed, "Lord, just let me speak once more, long enough to tell him I love him. I need to let him know that I am ready to go if that's Your will."

I waited. Nothing! I could not reach out. I could not tell my family of my love or readiness.

Pastor Bob remained by my side with the family. When it was time for the tracheotomy he came over and spoke to me. "Dorothy, because of the fluids gathering in your lungs, the doctors must perform a tracheotomy. That means they must insert a tube into your throat and attach it to a machine which will suction the fluid from your lungs. You are very weak, and it's possible you may not survive the surgery. The doctors will be as quick and as careful as they can be." He hesitated a moment, and then continued. "Are you ready? That's the most important question just now."

I appreciated his love and concern. I tried desperately with my eyes to convey to him and the family that all was well with my soul. Somehow, I felt they understood.

The experience that followed was unforgettable.

The surgical tools were brought into the room. Doctors and nurses robed in pale green gowns and caps worked quickly and efficiently.

"We can't anesthetize her," Dr. Strouth said quietly.

Suddenly I felt a terrible burning sensation in my neck. They made a small incision. I was aware of a snipping sound as they cut through the tracheal rings. The next thing I heard was an odd whooshing sound as wet air escaped from the hole in my neck. Then there was a searing pain. I felt fluid spraying out into the air, and a tiny catheter was inserted. Beads of cold perspiration rose on my forehead.

"God, how much more can I stand?" I was aware that the nurses connected the tube to a machine standing by my bed. "What was that? Would it hurt too?"

The machine began to work. I could feel the suction pulling the secretions out of my lungs. Relief flooded over me. Breathing became a little easier.

Slowly, I became aware of those around me. I could see the relief in their faces. Vince reached out and gently held my hand as I drifted into sleep.

I was still alive!

Chapter 6
Dark Days

My days didn't change much for some time. Breathing remained difficult, requiring constant care. The expense of special nursing care was financially out of the question, so family members took turns spending long hours at my bedside.

It was more than a vigil they kept. Each one was required to learn the process of using the suction machine. The nurses taught them how far to run the long tube into the hole in my throat, and how to extract the life-threatening fluid. This was often a frightening experience for both of us.

Because I appeared unresponsive, I overheard conversations that weren't meant for me to hear. Oh, I knew the family was aware that I was alert, but the nurses and other visitors seemed to think that because I could not respond I could not understand.

"Dorothy is very weak today. I'm afraid she may not be with us long," I heard a nurse whisper to a visitor. "Make your stay short so you won't tire her."

Many visitors were unprepared for the change in me. My weight had dropped sixty pounds, and I was now an emaciated eighty-five pounds. My face was pale, my eyes sunken, and the unsightly hole in my throat made strange, wet breathing sounds. My visitors often backed away, gasped, and ran from the room.

I wanted to shout after them, "Please come back. I'm still here, and I need you to know that I'm still the same person." Most never returned. My heart ached.

Others reacted differently and spent long hours at my bedside, making conversation or just sitting quietly beside me. They often encouraged me with stories of miracles they had read about or had witnessed. I fed on the slightest encouragement.

Vince and the family, especially, talked to me, keeping me up on the latest events at home. "Dorothy, I want to tell you what happened the other day," he would say, or, "You should have seen what the boys did today." I hungrily listened to them tell about all the things I longed to hear: about the family, the world, the church, and especially about my boys. But most of all I needed to know that Vince still loved and needed me. I clung to every word he spoke.

As they talked to me they gently rubbed my arms and legs, soothing out some of the racking pain. Their tender love and attention gave me courage to keep trying when giving up would have been so much easier.

Pastor Bob was a constant encouragement, always available. At one point he fasted and prayed seven days for my healing. On one of his daily visits he asked the nurses to help him hold me upright. My faith soared, though my body failed. When they held me up, my knees actually bent backward.

"Her knees! Watch out, her knees are bending backward," my sister Lena screamed.

"How will her legs ever hold her up?" another asked.

"She'll be all right; you just wait and see," Pastor Bob chattered encouragingly. "We'll keep working. You'll see a change."

The nurses looked doubtful, and a little disgusted. After that, when Pastor Bob visited, the nurses cast knowing glances at each other. "What do you suppose he'll try to get her to do today?" they whispered.

"This is good for me," I thought. "Can't they see? I'm alive! I can see. I can feel. I need this encouragement." I longed to say these things, but I remained hopelessly silent.

As Vince came each day, I could see the terrible strain he was under. He was weary from the long days and short nights. I was acutely aware of the sacrifices he and others were making, and loved them for it. But I could not tell them so.

Because I tried so hard to communicate with Vince, I invariably became worse at each of his visits. The fluid filled my lungs much faster from my efforts to speak, and I had to be suctioned more frequently. Mom's visits had somewhat the same effect on me. I had a difficult time controlling my emotions when she was with me. I wanted to say, "Mom, I appreciate your standing by me when most people thought I was a sympathy-seeker. I wish I could tell you how much I love you." My silence only heightened the anguish in her face that she tried so desperately to hide.

My frustration at not being able to express myself eventually led the nurses to caution me that if I didn't relax when Mom and Vince came, they would have to limit their visits. I tried desperately to stay calm after that.

As one day faded into the next, it became difficult to distinguish between night and day. My breathing was so labored that it became the most important thing in my life. "Keep breathing; just keep breathing," I told myself. I listened for the gurgling sound as each breath sent a wet spray from my lungs through the hole in my throat. I strained to see if the person watching me was still awake. Would they know when it was time to use the suction machine? How could I tell them when I couldn't breathe past the fluid any longer?

When I began to panic the fluid gathered more rapidly, causing the ones caring for me to scurry for the nurse or run the machine themselves.

I watched fearfully to see which nurse would come. Some were gentle and understanding. Others were harsh and careless, causing such anxiety that the simple procedure of suctioning my lungs became extremely painful, often causing blood to surface into the tube. I was grateful to those who took the time to be gentle.

As I grew even weaker, it became harder and harder for the suction machine to keep the fluid from my lungs. I was sure the doctor had given up on me. I could see that the family and Vince were exhausted from playing this waiting game. It began to seem to me that my life just wasn't worth the effort.

I was tired too. How much better it would be for Vince if I

just gave up. He could live again, spend time with the boys. I wasn't any good to him or to my family. I was growing certain that I would never be of any use again.

"I'm so tired, Lord. Can't You see how tired I am? I've done the best I can, but I just can't fight any longer."

Chapter 7
Telling the Boys

As Vince arrived at the hospital late one afternoon, he heard someone behind him, calling his name. It was Dr. Strouth, hurrying to stop him before he reached my door.

Vince turned wearily to face him. He couldn't help wondering what bad news was in store for him this time.

"I'd like to talk to you in the conference room, Vince."

How many times in the last month Vince had followed the doctor into that room! How many times had he sat stiffly in his chair, his stomach churning but his mind refusing obstinately to accept defeat. He hated the room's spotlessness, its sterility. It was a cold, impersonal place, where people with kind voices kept telling him terrible things about his wife.

What would it be this time? Vince sat stiffly on the edge of his chair, not wanting the doctor to start speaking. As long as there was no news at all, he could manage to keep going. He could hope.

"The time has come, Vince—" The doctor stopped and cleared his throat. "The time has come for you to prepare the boys for the probability that their mother is not coming home."

Vince felt for the arms of the chair. "What?" He asked dumbly. When there was no answer, he slowly stood up. "Have you really given up for sure this time?" he whispered.

Dr. Strouth nodded. "I'm afraid so, Vince. It's been touch and go before, but this time I don't see how she can make it through the night."

The colorless walls of the room closed around Vince until he wasn't sure he could get his breath. He struggled to make his voice work. "You're not positive," he pleaded.

"You're not listening to me, Vince. The time has come for you to face reality. I've been watching you, and I know that you're still clinging to some kind of vague hope that Dorothy will recover. I understand, and I sympathize. But the fact is that Dorothy is much weaker. It's going to take a miracle to pull her through this time. Vince, you've got to prepare your sons."

Vince wiped his hand across his eyes. When he spoke, it was as if to himself. "How can I tell them? How can I?"

Suddenly he couldn't stand being in that tiny room a moment longer. He thanked the doctor for his time, turned and left the room, and walked slowly down the hall. He walked aimlessly out to the parking lot, trying to remember where he had parked the car. He finally found it and got in. For some time he just sat there, confusing thoughts racing across his mind. How could he ever find the right words to tell the boys that their mother was going to die? And what then?

Alan was already beginning to have trouble in school. It wasn't just his grades that were down. His self-confidence was slipping. For some unknown reason he seemed to be trying to carry the blame for his mother's illness.

The more withdrawn Alan was, the more aggressive his brother Rick became. They were two opposites, pushed to extremes. The conflict that resulted almost daily made a difficult situation even worse.

Denny, who thought he could lick the world, and had always smiled when he said so, was developing anger, and with this anger came a fear that he wouldn't talk about and couldn't control.

Vince drove home, hardly aware of the direction he took. He entered the house, feeling the emptiness that always met him these days. Now the loneliness was going to be permanent, he thought—a vacuum inside him that would never be filled. He sat down wearily in a chair and waited, searching for words he could use when he talked to his sons. But his mind was blank. He needed help, and he knew whom to call.

Reaching for the phone, he dialed Pastor Bob's number.

"I need your help," he managed to say. "Can you come over to the house tonight? The boys have to be told that Dorothy isn't coming home."

He could hear the shock in the pastor's voice.

"Oh, Vince, has it come to that? Is the doctor really sure?"

"It's no use, Bob. The doctor says that without a real miracle she won't make it through the night. I have to prepare the boys, and I just can't do it alone." He couldn't talk any longer. He put the phone in its cradle and sat alone in the empty house while tears ran down his cheeks.

That evening he didn't tell the boys that the pastor was coming. Instead, he tried to listen to them and initiate activities that would keep them busy.

Presently the doorbell rang, and Rick ran to open it. He turned and shouted, "Hey, Dad, Pastor Bob is here."

"Ask him to come in," Vince said.

Pastor Bob didn't waste any time. He was wise enough to know that the sooner he could tell the boys, the better it would be for everyone.

"Gather 'round, boys," he said. "We have some serious things to discuss." His voice was grave, and the boys became quiet immediately.

"It's about your mother," Pastor Bob said.

"Is she worse?" All three seemed to ask the question.

"I'm afraid so. The doctor has told your dad that she may not live through the night."

Alan broke away from Vince's arms. "It's not true!" he shouted, then turned to his father. "Dad, tell us it isn't true," he pleaded.

"Maybe the doctor made a mistake!" Rick broke in.

"Yeah. Doctors have been wrong before," Denny said.

Vince shook his head. "I know how you feel. We're all trying to find some hope to cling to. But there isn't any. Not anymore."

"Wait a minute, Vince," Pastor Bob said. "I believe we can still trust in God's power to change things." He stretched out his arms as if to include them all. "We'll kneel down together right now and pray for her and ask God to spare her life. But we must remember that if it is His will to take her, that will be a blessing too. You know how much she has been suffering, and God may want to take her away from her pain." He looked at each boy in turn. "You wouldn't want to keep her here if she has to suffer, would you?"

All three boys slowly shook their heads, though tears were running down their faces. They all knelt together. It was a prayer of surrender that they shared. But as they prayed, Vince couldn't help wondering how he would manage alone.

When Pastor Bob had gone home and the boys were finally in bed, Vince had Mary, our neighbor, watch the boys while he returned to the hospital, where he and the family kept a silent vigil through the night. As the morning light sent the sun dancing across the quiet room, cautious excitement filled the room, for I was still alive. Indeed it was a miracle!

The boys were ecstatic when Vince called them with the news. Pastor Bob joined Vince at the hospital, and together with the family they spent a tearful, but joyful time thanking God for another day, another chance.

Chapter 8
The Promise

Three sinister visitors were never far from my room: Discouragement, Despair, and Self-pity.

Discouragement stalked in whenever he sensed that my weakness had allowed a moment of doubt to cross my mind. I even envisioned sad red eyes peering at me behind a ghostly white face as he wrapped a blanket of gloom around my heart. I thought about the sacrifices my family was making.

"Surely your sisters must be weary of all this," he whispered hoarsely.

I thought about Lena, working all night, driving twenty-five miles to Boise, and caring for me throughout the day. Sometimes she went without sleep for forty-eight hours at a time. Then there was Leona, who drove more than 200 miles, leaving her own family to come and stay with me. Vi came all the way from northern Idaho so that she, too, could help.

Gratitude swept over me as I thought of the sacrifices they were making.

"What about Vince?" Discouragement spoke again. The thoughts he conjured up were ugly and menacing. His red eyes and sinister grin drove me to Despair.

"Your family is crowding him out. They say he may not be doing all that can be done. What about that?"

Despair came in to sap what strength I had left. "The doctor has given up on you. You're tired. You can't fight any longer," he said, taunting me. I could almost see his beady, deep-set eyes looking deep into my soul.

"Besides," Self-pity joined in, "wouldn't it be better for Vince if you just gave up and died? That would free him from this terrible struggle. You're a burden. Yes, a burden." His voice was soft and enticing.

One night as I battled these unseen forces, I was so weak the doctor suggested that the family not stay, and he provided a special nurse to care for me. She was kind and caring. Her concern and understanding were like a warm shield of love surrounding me, lifting me above the enemies that plagued me. After caring for my needs, the nurse sat close beside me, constantly aware of my shallow breathing.

As I lay there, I began to realize that the strength I needed to continue breathing was ebbing from me. Every gurgling breath required a tremendous amount of energy, energy I no longer possessed. The pain in my body was intense. My lungs were heavy with fluid. I could fight no longer. I felt life slipping away, and I no longer cared.

"Oh, Father," I prayed, "I'm ready. If I can't get well, let me go now."

Suddenly, a great peace engulfed me. I felt the presence of God so close that had I been able to move my arms, it seemed that I could have reached out and touched Him. Words cannot describe the joy that I felt. I did not see a body or a person. I just sensed His presence at my side. I heard no words—not even a "still small voice," yet somehow I felt that He was communicating with me. A sense of wholeness flooded my mind.

God seemed to be giving me a choice. While I heard no words, it was almost as though He were saying to me, "Dorothy, you have asked Me to let you go now. Do you want that, or do you want to return to your family?"

Right then I wanted nothing more than to stay in His presence. For the first time in years I felt completely free of pain. And the peace of His presence was so beautiful that even though I could see and hear nothing, I wanted to stay there forever.

Then suddenly my feelings changed. I was overwhelmed with a desire to be well again and to be with Vince and the boys, to laugh with them and cry with them, to fix their breakfast and wash their clothes and clean the house for them. I wanted to go camping with them again, to sit beside them in church. I wanted to hug my boys, and I wanted to feel Vince's embrace, the warmth of his body close to mine.

Again, I felt that God was communicating with me. "Dorothy," He seemed to say—though still I heard no words and saw no Being—"you will indeed walk again, and you will be able to raise your boys."

I realized that in His own special way, God had given me a promise. He promised me that the terrible paralysis I was suffering at the present time would be removed. I would get well! What else could He mean by telling me, "You will be able to raise your boys"?

Love for Vince and the boys suddenly engulfed my entire being. I knew that I was feeling His love for them as well as my own. I so desired to stay in His presence. I felt such peace and well-being there, but I desired more to do His will.

I began struggling back to consciousness. Once more I became aware of the room around me and the nurse sitting quietly beside me. I had no way to explain this experience, but I sensed that this night would soon end and again I would live. Improvement was certainly not immediately evident. I'm glad I did not know how long the struggle would be.

The nurse was unaware of my experience. I could tell no one, yet I believed I would walk again, return home, and live to raise my sons. I never doubted this fact.

I wish I could say that the pain left immediately and that my struggle to breathe eased somewhat, but this was not the case. In fact, the doctors could not understand how I continued to live. In their opinion, even if my lungs eventually cleared, the nerves had deteriorated to the point that they would never carry messages again. The doctor told Vince that even if I were ever able to exercise again and regain muscle tone, the deteriorated nerves were beyond restoration. They gave little hope of recovery.

However, my inner hope sustained me, even when physical improvement was not evident. I hung on and waited for the promise. I desperately longed for immediate healing. I fought

Despair again and again as he cajoled me into thinking it had all been a hope-induced dream. I again began asking Why, and Despair stepped up the battle.

"Lord, why is it taking so long? Please give me some indication that healing is taking place so that I can have the courage to continue this tiring struggle."

Intravenous feeding had been my only sustenance for some time. One day, shortly after I had asked for a sign, a nurse bustled into my room with a tray. Sitting on the tray was a shimmering, jiggling bowl of red Jello. "Hi, Dorothy. How about you and me trying something different today?" she said as she began rolling up the head of my bed. "Look, I've brought you some Jello to try. Doesn't it look good?"

Oh, yes! It really did look good. It had been so long since I had tasted food. I had never realized how fragrant Jello was. Though apprehensive, I eagerly waited for that first bite. She carefully placed a spoonful into my mouth. I choked! Each time she tried, my throat refused to accept it.

"Please don't give up!" I wanted to say to her. It tasted s-o-o-o good.

She did not give up. She patiently continued with small amounts until finally it began going down without the choking. I knew God had heard and answered my prayer!

With added nourishment I began to gain strength, and with added strength I was soon able to use facial gestures to convey my needs. I even began to move my mouth enough to form words, although no sound came out.

Breathing became a bit easier, so I began to think of something besides my breathing. I began to think about home and my boys. The more I thought, the more I believed that if I could go home for only a few minutes, surely I would improve. I began mouthing the word *home* every time anyone looked at me. Finally Vince mentioned this to the doctor.

"Oh, no, Dorothy. You're not ready for that for a long time yet," he told me as he examined me one day.

I persisted in my plea until at last, with trepidation, the doctor decided I could go home for a very short time. I had no idea of the work entailed in such a venture. All I knew was that I needed to be home again, to see that the boys were OK, and to strengthen their belief, and mine, that I would one day be well again.

This was very trying for Vince. He made arrangements to borrow a delivery van with enough room for my wheelchair and the suction machine. I still needed to be suctioned approximately every twenty minutes, more often if I became too excited. He was terribly afraid that something would go wrong and my slight improvement would be reversed. Nevertheless, they prepared me for the trip home.

How good it felt to sit upright as they placed me into a wheelchair, fastening me in tightly. For the first time in weeks, I was able to see more than the small piece of the visible world from my hospital bed. I was so excited I could hardly breathe. For the first time in months I really felt alive as we left the hospital.

It seemed an eternity since I had felt the warm breath of the sun's rays or smelled the fragrance of the flowers blooming along the sidewalk. I knew again the kiss of the breeze. I gazed at the blue sky, the white clouds, and the birds flying overhead. I heard the laughter of children playing in the yards. The laughter, the birds, and the breeze were like an orchestra playing just for me. I thanked God. "My God, my God, how I thank You for bringing me this far, for giving me strength enough to go home again!"

The family was waiting when we reached the house. The boys and others who had not seen me for some time registered shocked surprise at my appearance, though they tried valiantly not to show it.

Alan, Rick, and Dennis all began talking at once, each one trying to catch me up on the latest. Oh, how I had missed them!

I became so emotional from the excitement of seeing my boys, my mother, and other family members, that my lungs began to fill, and the suction machine was soon needed. Some of the family began questioning the wisdom of allowing me to come home.

Silently I prayed for strength and calmness so I would not have to return to the hospital so soon. Prayer brought results, and I was able to stay a while longer. Soon, however, it was time to return. How I hated to leave, but I was becoming very weary, and I knew that I must return to the security of my hospital room.

One day a friend, Cassie Knudsen, visited me in the hospital. Anxious to share some hope, she related to me the story of a friend who, being unable to walk, had gone to the Elks Rehabilitation Hospital. There she was soon helped to walk again. I remembered this and began dreaming of going to the Elks, where I was sure they would help me to walk and talk again. I began trying to communicate this to Vince, the doctor, anyone whose attention I could get. It became the uppermost thought on my mind. I should have known that the Lord was preparing the way.

Chapter 9
The Elks

Another day, another conference! It seemed as if every time Vince met with the doctor he had more distressing news. This time, as so many times before, it required more decision making.

"The hospital staff is requesting that you begin searching for a nursing home or a care center to place Dorothy in," the doctor began. "There really is nothing more the hospital can do for her. There's little hope that she will ever be able to care for herself. You must know that. I know she has made some improvement, but it is so slight, and the expenses are mounting so rapidly, that you just must think of an alternative."

"Surely there's a facility somewhere that will do more than just make her comfortable," Vince said. "Isn't there someone that can help?"

"I have contacted the University of Washington Medical School, where research on porphyria is being done," Doctor Strouth replied. "I hope that may be our answer. I have not received a reply from them yet."

"If you think there is any chance, I will try to find a way to get her there," Vince said with cautious excitement.

With the doctor's promise to keep trying, Vince began making arrangements.

A few days later, however, Dr. Strouth telephoned Vince. "I'm so sorry," he said, "but the medical school in Seattle has refused to accept Dorothy. They say they cannot care for anyone as dependent on twenty-four hour care as she is. I know how much you were counting on this." The doctor was apologetic. After all his endeavor, Vince was heartsick. "Do you have any ideas, Doctor? Dorothy has been bugging everyone about the Elks. Is that a possibility?" he asked in desperation. "We could try," Dr. Strouth answered. "However, they may not be able to supply the care she needs either."

Vince immediately visited the staff there. Sensing his desperation they finally agreed, but only on a trial basis. My continuing there would depend on the progress I made.

I remember very little of the move to the Elks. I only recall waking up in unfamiliar surroundings. The sounds, smells, and atmosphere told me that something was very different. I became aware of the brightness of the room and turned my eyes slowly as far as I could in the direction of the light. I saw a large window from which streaks of early-morning sun came glittering across the ceiling, sending dancing reflections across the stark white walls, making the room alive with light.

Suddenly a nurse's cheery voice broke into my reverie. "Well, well, good morning, Mrs. Shell. How are you this morning?"

I moved my eyes in the direction of her voice.

As she rearranged my pillow and straightened the bed she could see my confusion. "You are at the Elks Rehabilitation Hospital," she said cheerfully, and began to explain the new routine. "We are going to try to help you get well. Do you understand? We will be giving you therapy classes to get these arms and legs moving. In the afternoons and on weekends you may rest and have visitors."

All the time she was talking she bustled around, checking the suction machine and taking my pulse and temperature.

"At last I'm at the Elks!" I thought gratefully. "Now, I'm sure I'll get well."

The days bustled with activity that I was not used to. This helped them to pass more quickly than the dull days at the hospital.

By now family and friends found it more difficult to stay with me through the nights. I lay in the darkness feeling frightened and alone. The halls echoed the quietness as I lay awake, reluctant to sleep for fear no one would hear when my breathing became labored. My body continued to ache with pain from lying in one position. It was a relief to welcome the first gray streaks of dawn through my window each morning. My spirits rose in anticipation of afternoon visits from family and friends, and the encouragement of Pastor Bob.

The days were an endless parade of routine activities, some pleasant, others painful. The first thing on the agenda was bath time. Occasionally it, too, was painful. Even so it felt good to have someone caring for me after the long night of terror. After my bath I was wheeled into therapy.

Therapy class was grueling and long. In the first weeks, I watched with great anticipation as the therapist moved my legs and arms back and forth, up and down. The thought of possible improvement filled my every waking hour. Later came a feeling of defeat when my muscles failed to respond. I tried to concentrate on the exercise, but it began to seem so pointless. There was no noticeable sign of improvement.

"Come on, Dorothy, push, push! Try harder! Are you trying?" the therapist prodded.

"Yes, I'm trying! God knows how hard I'm trying," I wanted to shout as I was pushed to my limits.

Each time I prayed, "Go, hands, go!" But nothing happened. Over and over I tried to send a message, but the message never got through. I grew weary and discouraged.

The frustration and disappointment became obvious on the therapist's face. In my own frustration I wanted to lash out at him, "Let me alone. I'm tired, and I don't want to try anymore." I longed to say these things, but I could only cry.

Again Discouragement and Self-pity began to sow seeds of doubt.

"Lord, why is it taking so long?" I wailed inwardly. "You promised. I *know* You promised!"

After therapy, I was wheeled through the exercise gym on the way to the pool. There I saw others learning to walk with artificial limbs or exercising partial limbs. They were doing all the things I could not do. I felt an overpowering jealousy of even those whose limbs were deformed or missing. They could still do something! I could do nothing. I wrapped myself in gloom.

In the pool, I was placed on a mat and lowered into the water. It felt warm, comforting, and soothing. The motion of the water against my lifeless body gave the illusion that my legs and arms were moving on their own. Feeling free, as if I could swim away, I dared to hope that I would recover.

Trying to help me become more self-sufficient, the therapists devised a gadget that fit on the arm of my wheelchair to help me begin to learn to feed myself. My arm fit into the appliance, and a fork-spoon type utensil was attached to my hand with an elastic band. As they pushed my shoulder and arm forward, the spoon swooped down toward the plate on my tray, scooping up the food—that is, if I was lucky enough to hit it right. As the shoulder continued to move forward, the spoon came up toward my mouth. If my luck held, I would hit my mouth. Unfortunately, this did not often happen, and the food ended up in my lap.

Learning to feed myself like this was one of the most trying feats I had to do. Occasionally, I became so exasperated after repeated failures that I refused to try. Finally they would feed me. Later I could be coaxed into trying again, until I managed to achieve a smoother movement. These small successes brightened my otherwise discouraging days.

Afternoons were filled with visits from family and friends. I looked forward eagerly to visits from Alan, Rick, and Denny. I could hear them come tearing down the hall to my room long before I was able to see them. I was always eager to hear any news they had to tell.

"Mom, you should see the frogs we have," they exclaimed one day as they entered my room. "We're keeping them in the window well at home."

"Yeah, and we caught a ground squirrel too. He almost got away, but we caught him. Dad even built him a cage," they told me proudly.

One day Rick came back after some time of exploration. "Look, Mom, gloves!' He held his hands out for me to see. Horrors! They were covered with a wax film from fingertips to elbows. My heart sank. What had he been into?

"One of the nurses let me stick my arms into the big vat of

wax they have in the therapy room," he explained, laughing. "It feels funny."

I worried that they might make a nuisance of themselves, but their enthusiasm was good medicine.

By this time the boys no longer worried that I would die, but I knew the pressure they were under. Summertime was very difficult for them. They were shuffled from one relative to another. They were in continuous change. I prayed daily for their safekeeping.

My failure to respond to treatment far outweighed my success, and one day a staff meeting was called to discuss my case. There was only one therapist who felt that there was enough progress to warrant keeping me in the Elks. "Please, let me try a little longer," she argued. "I know it seems hopeless, but there has been a little improvement. She can at least partially feed herself. I believe she can be helped."

The director broke in. "The consensus from everyone else is that the improvement is too slight. Our hospital is understaffed, and she requires too much care. I don't see how we can justify keeping her here at the expense of admitting someone who has more chance of recovery. The doctors think the nerve damage is irreversible. I'm really sorry. There's nothing more we can do."

The decision was made. The next day they would tell Vince.

Chapter 10
Sent Home to Die

Vince sat stunned, trying to cope with another rejection, as the director of the Elks Rehabilitation Hospital told him they would no longer be able to care for me. The old feeling of despair was back again. The words kept ringing in his ears. "I'm sorry, Mr. Shell, there is nothing more we can do. Your wife just isn't responding to the treatments. She remains gravely ill, and Dr. Strouth indicates that there is little hope that she can survive much longer. Further treatments are not advised at this time."

After months of prayer and struggle to help me hang on, they too now insisted that Vince place me elsewhere.

"Please, you can't give up too," Vince pleaded. "You can't send her home like this." He begged them to reconsider.

"I'm sorry," the director said. "There just isn't any more we can do but make her comfortable, and we have such a long list of patients waiting for treatment. The room is desperately needed for someone else."

In desperation, Vince talked with Dr. Strouth again about what he thought the future held for us.

"What they told you at the Elks Rehabilitation Hospital is true, Vince," Dr. Strouth said. "I don't see Dorothy improving any from the near vegetable state she is presently in, and in all probability she will eventually die from the build-up of fluids in her lungs or from heart failure due to the extra pressure on her heart."

Again faced with defeat, Vince knew he must make more decisions. The expense of nursing-home care was too great. He decided to buy the necessary equipment and care for me himself at home.

Vince was fearful and frustrated as he came for me that day. Frantic questions crossed his troubled mind. "How can I take care of an invalid wife and three boys? How can I keep up with my job and do all this too? Who will care for Dorothy during the day? Where will I find the money to hire help? What if she dies like they say she might? Lord, help me. Why, Lord, why?"

I could see the apprehension in his eyes, though he tried to hide it. He faced another mountain, and he had little energy left to begin the climb.

I, too, felt his frustration. The feeling of hopelessness was overpowering. "Maybe I should not have clung to life so desperately," I thought, remembering the time I nearly died. "Maybe it would have been easier for Vince to lose me than to take me home like this." Love and concern for Vince and the knowledge of the burden I was putting on him made my heart ache. Again my mind returned to the time during my desperate fight for life when the promise that I would indeed walk and talk again had been given to me, but today I desperately needed assurance.

Leaving the Elks at last, I was excited to go home once again, but inside my whole being wanted to shout, "What is going to happen to me? Who will suction out my lungs? Who will care for me? I am so afraid!"

I was completely dependent on people and machines to perform every bodily function. The inability to speak, and the anxiety this caused, left me exhausted. My mind remained alert even though my body was weak and paralyzed. I had no way to convey my fears to anyone.

The nurse patiently began showing Vince how to care for the tracheotomy and the suction machine. "Just remember, her lungs still need to be suctioned about every twenty minutes," she said. "I'll also give you a quick rundown on what to do daily for exercises and her other bodily needs."

Vince awkwardly followed all her instructions while she watched. I could see how hard it was for him, how frightened he was of not being able to care for me properly. The results would be fatal should he fail to awaken on time.

The quiet bustle of someone else going through the motions of preparing me for my journey home was unnerving. My heart pounded so strongly that I was sure everyone could hear its wild throbbing. I looked around the room, taking in the stark whiteness of the walls and bed, the antiseptic odors that permeated the air. Mostly I remembered how the early morning sun shimmered across the room, bringing life to each new day. It was a room where I had spent days of struggle, trying to regain lost motion, fighting for life itself. Endless days that had turned into weeks and months. Suddenly, I didn't want to leave!

"I feel safer here," I thought. "Even the sickly hospital odors and the squeaky wheels of carts in the hallway that have annoyed me so seem like good smells and sounds now." The day I had prayed and longed for had come, and I was afraid.

"Well, Honey, are you ready? Let's go home," Vince announced as he came into the room with the wheelchair he had purchased for me.

Gently he lifted my eighty-pound body into the wheelchair. I sat motionless, staring straight ahead. I wanted to reach out for his hand. I longed to hold him in my arms once more. If I could only smooth away the lines of worry that were so prevalent in his face now. He had been so good to me, so patient and understanding as he stayed by my side through this long, trying ordeal. Love and gratitude overwhelmed me.

"If only I could tell him, if only!" But I could not utter a word, or even take his hand. The paralysis was still too complete. I was an island unto myself.

Shivering with the full understanding of this, and the realization of the burden I would be to him daily, I wondered if it could be done. It seemed impossible, but we trusted in a God who loves doing the impossible. He would not forsake us now.

Filled with a million unexpressed feelings that alternated between fear and hope, I was finally going home, but I realized that most people thought I was being sent home to die.

Chapter 11
Home Again

Some days are never to be forgotten. The day I left the Elks seemed a day of defeat. After so many months of struggle and uncertainty, now to go home like this, completely dependent on others, seemed like labor in vain. Faith and hope wrestled against the hard medical facts.

The twentieth day of August 1964, will be forever engraved on my mind. It would ordinarily have been a special day of celebration. It was our fourteenth wedding anniversary and our son, Rick's birthday, but I was going home a hopeless invalid.

Going home, and on such a special day, should have been a time of rejoicing, but instead, I was scared stiff.

As Vince wheeled me down the long corridor toward our waiting car, I wanted to shout, "Please wait! Don't give up on me. Please, won't somebody try to help me?" No words came. Only frightening thoughts.

The nurses helped Vince put me into the front seat of the car, propping me up with pillows to keep me from falling. Then they loaded the faithful old suction machine, with all its attachments. Finally, we were on our way.

I nearly toppled over at every turn as we traveled home. Each time my body fell forward, Vince reached over and pushed me up again. My helplessness angered me. "Why did I have to go home like this, anyway?" I complained inwardly. "Why couldn't I be normal like everyone else?"

I was so engrossed in just trying to stay erect that I scarcely noticed what a beautiful sunshiny day it was. I was only vaguely aware of the gentle summer breeze that blew across my face through the open car window. But as we neared our house my excitement began to mount. Suddenly, I was terribly homesick. I couldn't get there fast enough! I strained my eyes to catch the first glimpse of home. It had never looked so beautiful! The lawn was like green velvet, contrasted by the red and yellow roses blooming along the drive.

Then, in the doorway, I saw the boys, waiting and waving. Standing in front of the big picture window was my mom, and, oh yes, there was Verla, my youngest sister, and Vi, Lena, and others I could not clearly make out. What a heartwarming sight. My loving, helpful family were all there to welcome me home. Maybe, just maybe, everything would be all right after all.

Then, the realization that the drastic change in my physical appearance might be difficult for the boys hit me unexpectedly. How would they react? At the Elks they had expected it, but to come home this way was much different. With my drastic weight loss, there was certainly nothing attractive left of me. The gaping hole in my neck still made wet, repulsive sounds as I breathed.

"Turn the car around. I don't want to go home like this," I wanted to cry out. Vince was unaware of my anxiety.

Alan, Rick, and Dennis flew down the walk the greet me as the car pulled into the driveway. I couldn't turn to look at them, nor even muster an answering smile. I wanted so desperately to throw open the car door and gather them in my arms. But all I could do was sit there staring straight ahead and wait.

For a moment, the boys looked shocked as they reached the car, but only for a moment. Then they threw open the car door yelling, "Mom, Mom! Welcome home, Mom!"

Family and friends came running from the house, echoing the welcome home. Vince lifted me out of the car and into the wheelchair. The boys began to argue about who would get to wheel me into the house.

"Oh, God, thank You for home!" My heart was full of gratitude as I looked at my living room, now filled with warmth and laughter. After months in sterile hospital rooms, the room looked so beautiful. The pictures on the wall, the vases filled with colorful flowers, the knickknacks on the shelves were like old, familiar friends.

I listened to the excited buzz of conversation. It was frustrating to hear people talking all around me and be unable to turn my head in the direction of the speaker, and worse yet, not be able to respond. As frustration mounted, so did the fluid in my lungs. I panicked.

However, Vince immediately sensed the problem, and a calmness came over me as he began to set up the suction equipment. In the bedroom, he gently lifted me from the wheelchair and placed me on the hospital bed that he had set up for me and started the suctioning process. Had the situation been different, I would have chuckled at the sight of the boys standing wide-eyed beside my bed. They reminded me of little birds, leaning toward the edge of the nest in anticipation of a parent bringing home a worm. They stood in awe as they watched Vince start the machine.

Suddenly Dennis became alarmed. "Dad, what are you doing? You're hurting Mom."

"Keep still, Dennis," Alan spoke. "Dad knows what he's doing."

"Dad wouldn't hurt Mom, and you know it," Rick chimed in.

It must have been a strange sight as they watched Vince run the long tube through the hole in my neck. Soon sucking sounds filled the room. Rick was fascinated by the fluid that bubbled up through the clear plastic tube and flowed into the glass container.

"Yuck! look at this! Where's it coming from?"

Questions tumbled from their lips one after another.

Patiently, Vince explained the suction procedure to the boys as he completed the task.

As my breathing again became easier, I noticed a strange apparatus attached to the side of my bed. Aware of my curiosity, Vince explained that he and John, his cousin, had gone to the Elks and had observed the equipment that was used for my exercise therapy. Being quite inventive themselves, they built these devices on my bed in order that Vince might work with me as the therapists had done. He was determined to keep the muscles from atrophying by continuing the exercises they had shown him.

Vince was not about to admit defeat. Although God had not made His presence known to Vince the way He had to me, He certainly had given him the endurance, patience, and determination to keep on keeping on.

Out in the living room, my family was making plans for my home care. Friends offered to assist.

"I'll be responsible for the schedule and inform each one what day you should come," my sister-in-law, Wilma, said as she began putting down the names of all who volunteered. This task took a tremendous amount of time. It was a job well done.

The excitement of being home and seeing all the family finally became too much for me, and they began to leave one by one. We were alone at last, Vince, the boys, and I. However, the boys soon got tired of the one-way conversation and left to get ready for bed. Now Vince and I were left alone to ponder what lay ahead.

"How long would this nightmare last?" I wondered. "How does a family exist like this? How would it all end?"

Not wanting to be quiet long enough to face up to these questions and broken dreams, Vince soon busied himself preparing me for the long night ahead. He was constantly aware that he must now wake up every twenty or thirty minutes to clear my lungs with the suction machine.

"How can I be sure I will wake up at the right time?" he kept asking himself. "Lord, please help me to awaken in time. Without Your help I can't do all that I must do," he prayed.

I lay awake in the hospital bed at the foot of our own lovely bed while Vince prepared himself for sleep. I too worried if he would be able to wake up in time.

I looked around the bedroom. This room was special to both Vince and me. It was the room where we had shared our dreams for the future, had laughed, cried, loved and been loved in return, and once in a while had argued. I remembered nights I had cuddled up to him. Sometimes, when pain had kept me from sleeping, I had cuddled even closer. I always felt better just knowing he was there. His embrace, even in sleep, had thrilled and comforted me.

"How long will it be," I wondered, "before I will be able to leave this ugly old hospital bed and once again know the joy of being in Vince's arms?"

Self-pity threatened. I fought back the tears.

"Oh, God, please help this night to go by without incident," I prayed, as Vince turned out the lights and we both slept from exhaustion.

Chapter 12
Ministering Saints

"B-z-z-z-!"

I awoke with a start. "What is that. Where is it coming from?" I tried to turn. My body didn't respond. For one uneasy moment I was afraid that I was having another of those horrible nightmares. But the noise stopped. I realized that I was at home, and the old alarm clock had just gone off.

"Good morning, Honey. How's my girl today?" Vince said as he came over and kissed me. He put his strong arms around me, holding me close. His touch brought a mixture of agony and joy. The slightest touch still caused my nerve endings to react with intense pain. But oh, how good it felt to wake up in my own room and have Vince there to help me greet the new day.

The quietness of the moment was interrupted as the boys bounded into the bedroom. "Good morning, Mom," they shouted. "How do you feel today?"

It sounded so good to hear their happy voices. They crowded around the bed, smiling and patting my hand. I yearned to hold each one in my arms. Just to be home with them again would have to be enough for now.

Each morning the alarm went off at five-thirty. Vince fed the boys and got them ready for school. When they had left, he turned his attention to me. He fed me and prepared me for the day. As soon as the first "day-care" lady arrived, he left for work.

How relieved I was when the day-care lady arrived on time.

I knew that if she was late and I was left alone, I could drown with no one to use the suction machine. There were no words to express my gratitude to Cassie Knudsen, Hazel Groff, Mary Shell, and many, many others, who came daily to minister to my needs.

The day passed slowly. Hazel chatted happily to me as she sat at my bedside, listening for the sounds that indicated that my lungs needed suctioning. When the time inevitably came, with fear and trembling, she gingerly fed the tube down the hole in my neck and started the machine. We both sighed with relief when the procedure was safely accomplished.

"Would you like me to read to you from the Bible?" she asked, looking for the response. Gradually, each one learned to "read" the signals I tried to send with my eyes. Sometimes during the long hours, the thought of my helplessness became overwhelming. When I couldn't hold back the tears, they would gently wipe them away and comfort me.

I always looked forward to three-thirty in the afternoon when the boys came home from school. As they ran up the walk and burst into the door, they shouted, "Hi, Mom, we're home!" I had forgotten how much like music boys' voices sounded. They stormed into my room with hugs and excited chatter. As quickly as they came, they left. I could hear them in the kitchen.

"May I have a peanut butter sandwich, Mom?" Dennis called, not really expecting an answer.

"Not me. I want ice cream," Rick cut in.

"Don't spoil your appetite for dinner," I wanted to call to them. But no words came. Only silent desperation.

Sometimes the day-care ladies stayed with me until Vince came home, but as the boys learned to care for me, they often left shortly after the boys got home. The boys were usually attentive and watched me carefully, but at times the call of outdoor play lured them away. I was frightened when left alone. I soon learned that they never forgot their duties and kept close watch to be sure I was all right. They learned to be aware of when I needed to be suctioned.

After a while, the strain of the responsibility began to take its toll. They quarreled, and at times came to blows. It was utter frustration to lie there and listen to them yelling and hitting one another, and not be able to say anything.

"I've just got to get up and settle this fight before they harm each other," I told myself. "But I can't. Oh, God, I can't!" Tears of despair rolled down my cheeks. I felt so useless.

Again I felt rejected and let down by God. "Why, God, why?" Deep inside I knew He was working a miracle in me, but doubts filled me when it seemed to take so long.

Each evening, Vince hurried home and plunged into the work to be done. There was little time for rest. Often, dinner was prepared by the day-care lady. Other evenings Vince had to do the cooking. While dinner was cooking, he spent time with the boys, playing ball or just listening to their accounts of the day. After dinner, the boys cleaned up the dishes while Vince fed me.

Feeding me was quite a procedure. I was quite content to let Vince feed me like a baby, but not so, Vince. He determined that I would do everything I could possibly do for myself. He refused to feed me until I had spent some time trying to feed myself with the feeding attachment that had been made for me at the Elks Hospital. How I hated that thing! Try as I would, I could not control it. If I tried to push it up to my mouth, the food invariably landed on my shoulder, in my nose, or on the floor. What a mess! Sometimes I gave up in despair and began to cry. Even crying was messy. Imagine crying without being able to clean your nose or wipe the tears away! It did bring results, however. Vince lovingly took over and fed me.

After dinner, the exercises began. Vince moved my legs and arms as he had observed the therapists doing. "Come on, Honey, let's move those legs! Way up now. Don't frown. Act like you are enjoying it, OK?"

Over and over again, up, down, in, out, rubbing and kneading my sore muscles, Vince exercised me until I thought I could not stand it any longer.

He never let up, always pushing, pushing. "Come on, Honey, try, try, try. You can do it. We'll make it work. Let's try again. Just one more time." His persistence never ceased.

After those interminable exercises, Vince cared for my personal needs. There was my bath and the distasteful job of the catheter bag that had to be emptied and cleansed. It was so good to have him close by, caring for me, but I was acutely aware of the horrendous job he had undertaken.

Each Saturday Vince drove me to a beauty shop operated by a friend, Charlotte Gates, and helped while she shampooed and cared for my hair. I looked forward to this day. It felt so-o-o good to have someone work with my aching, itching head, after lying so still so many hours.

Life at home soon became routine. I prayed daily for Vince, and God heard and answered those prayers. God gave him the strength and courage to continue working with me even after four months, when there seemed to be little visible progress.

"Honey, what's going on here? Your clothes are getting too small!" Vince exclaimed one morning as he was dressing me for the day. It was then we became aware that I was actually beginning to gain weight.

Soon after we discovered my weight gain I began to feel something happening to my muscles. Slowly at first, they began to respond. The response was so gradual that Vince didn't know when he began to do less and I began to do more. With new hope I began to look forward to the exercise I had grown to hate.

Feeding myself was also becoming easier. Instead of tossing the food over my shoulder or in my nose, I actually hit my mouth most of the time. This gave Vince a break from some of the responsibility.

Then, day of all days! Vince discovered that when he placed his finger over the hole in my throat I could breathe a few words audibly. With this discovery I could finally express myself. There is no way to put into words the joy we both felt. The boys were fascinated.

God's promise was unfolding, slowly at first, but when I breathed those first few words, still not much more than a whisper, I knew that God had heard and was answering our prayer. Not by our timing, but His.

As the progress became more evident and family and friends could see the change, they began to push me even harder, sometimes harder than I could tolerate.

Soon I, too, became obsessed with getting on with it. Now instead of the questions, "Why me?" I echoed, "Why not now?" The progress seemed so slow, and I was often impatient and cranky. It was then that Vince would remind me of how far I had come and how much I could already do. Anticipation of things to come soon overcame the agitation, and again, all our effort continued.

Chapter 13
Beginning to Live Again

Seven difficult months passed. Our family seemed to be adjusting to the circumstances in which we found ourselves. However, the boys began to have a hard time concentrating on their studies. I was unable to help them, and Vince was so involved with other responsibilities that he had little time to help.

As the boys' grades fell sharply, so did my spirits. I was heartbroken to realize that their problems were largely due to our home situation. It was hard for me not to feel guilty when I saw them struggle. However, as I progressed they seemed to adjust more, and as they adjusted, their grades improved. Perhaps we all grew a little during this time.

I don't know when I realized that I needed the suction machine less at night. Vince was able to sleep longer intervals, giving him more rest. Soon, my day-care ladies noticed the improvement. This indeed was cause to rejoice.

"Hi, Honey, how's my girl today?" were always Vince's first words when he came home from work. One evening he came home just too exhausted to cook. "Let's do something different tonight. Let's all go out to a restaurant to eat," he suggested.

The boys were ecstatic. I was scared stiff.

"How will Vince manage? What if I choke? What will people think?" I worried. However, excitement mounted within me as Vince dressed me for the excursion.

When Vince wheeled me into the cafe in my wheelchair, I became aware of heads turning and people staring. Vince noticed my reaction, so he leaned over and whispered to me,

"Don't let them bother you, Honey. Let's just enjoy ourselves."
I tried, but I could not miss the astonished stares of everyone.
I felt conspicuous and uneasy.

Vince, aware of my discomfort, smiled and took my hand.
"Don't worry about other people," he whispered. "We're here as
a family, and we're having a good time. They just don't understand." With that, he began making happy conversation. It was
all I could do to sit through our first meal out, with Vince feeding me. Later, I became less self-conscious and began to look
forward to eating out.

Often I thought about all that Vince was doing for me. I was
filled with gratitude and love. "How fortunate I am," I told
myself. "It wasn't by accident that Vince came my way. God
knew I would need someone special, and Vince is special indeed!"

Shortly after the restaurant venture, Vince surprised me on
Sunday morning. "Honey, today we are all going to church
together, OK?" Until now the boys were being picked up and
taken to church by Don and Hazel Groff. Hazel was one of my
day-care ladies. Today we were going as a family.

Vince and the boys scurried around. After I was bathed and
dressed, Vince began to comb my hair.

"That's not the way to do it!" I thought. He was trying hard
to make me feel and look normal. Although it was not the way
I would have done it, I appreciated his efforts.

What a tremendous thrill to be able to worship together with
my family and the church family that had been praying for my
recovery for so many months. What a blessing to be a part of
my church again!

Soon it was the Christmas season. It was difficult to become
excited about festivities. Before my paralysis I had enjoyed
hearing carols playing in the shops, the last-minute choir prac-
tices, the hustle and bustle of Christmas shopping. I would still
want to hear the carols telling the story, but I wanted to be in
on the rest too. I desperately wanted to buy Vince and the boys
a gift to show them my love, but I was sure there was no way.

My sisters, Lena and Vi, had other ideas. They came by one
day. "We want to help you shop for a gift for Vince and the

boys," they explained as they struggled to load the wheelchair into the trunk of their car.

Once downtown, I again felt the stares of pity and curiosity. Even so, I managed to concentrate on the purpose of the outing.

Since I could now mouth a few whispered words, I was able to indicate Yes or No to the selections of shirts for each one as my sisters patiently displayed them to me. After the shirts were gift wrapped they hurried home, fearing that I would soon need the suction machine. By the time we reached home I was completely exhausted, but the thrill of being part of the hustle and bustle was one of the most encouraging events in months.

Christmas morning the boys awoke at the crack of dawn, rushing up the stairs to see what gifts awaited them. They could hardly contain their excitement while Vince helped me get ready.

As soon as we had once again heard the wonderful story of Christ's birth and had thanked God for the progress I had made, the boys tore into their packages. They were surprised and pleased when they found a gift under the tree for each of them from me.

I had never been more aware of the gift of Christ than at this Christmas. As carols played on the record player, I was reminded of how close I had drawn to Christ during the trying months we had just struggled through.

The months that followed were exciting and memorable. I continued to gain weight, and my muscles responded more and more to the exercises that Vince administered daily. Although still unable to move them myself, I was building strength, and excitement mounted at each small improvement.

Each day I thought, "This is the day I will move my head or my hand or my legs." I began to picture myself well. I *expected* a miracle!

Vince began an all-out effort. "Come on, Honey. Push! push! I know you can do it!" he chided as he increased the exercises, prodding me on constantly. Slowly but surely, the muscles began to respond. Each new response brought a thrill of joy.

Vince bought devices to exercise my hands. "Try squeezing

this rubber ball," he told me one day, placing a sponge rubber ball between my hands. "Now, squ-e-e-eze! Come on, try harder—as hard as you can."

When I tired of squeezing the ball, he gave me a large rubber band with handgrips on each end and encouraged me to pull it.

"Good, Dorothy. That was good. Now try to pull again." Day after day, I struggled to make my hands do the work. It took tremendous concentration. As soon as I made progress with one exercise, Vince added a new one.

I was still very weak, and sometimes his exuberance was so exhausting, and I got so tired, that I would refuse to try any longer. He would slack off then, and later gently encourage me to try again.

"Honey, today we are going to try something new," he said to me on one of those days of trying new things. "You have been doing so well, I think you can stand now. Don't be afraid. Just do as I say. Easy now. I won't let you fall."

I was terribly afraid. "What if I fall?" I thought. I wasn't ready for this yet. I did my best to cooperate. Vince eased me to a standing position. My knees buckled immediately. He pulled me back up, supporting me with his body. Day after day we practiced. Just when I was ready to give up, my legs held my weight, just for an instant. We were jubilant! At each attempt thereafter, I grew stronger and less fearful.

One day Vince came home with a big smile. "Dorothy, I've brought a surprise for you," he said. He was as excited as if he were the one getting the surprise. He wheeled me into the living room. There in the middle of the room stood an exercise bike. "Now you can exercise your leg muscles on this," he said proudly. He tried lifting me onto the bike, and we both nearly fell over. I didn't have enough strength or balance to help. The bike seat was small, so it was a real achievement when we finally succeeded. The ordeal was so frightening to me that I might have refused to continue had the boys not gotten such a laugh from watching. They cheered as we made each attempt. This made me less apprehensive.

Once I was seated on the bike, Vince moved my feet up and

down on the pedals until one day I was able to move them a little by myself.

As I became more confident on the bike, Vince instructed Mary or one of the other day-care ladies on how to get me on the bike so I could spend time on it during the day. When he arrived home each evening, his first words were, "Hi, Honey, how's my girl today?" and immediately after that his second words were, "How many miles did you ride on the bike today? How many times did you pull the band?"

I began to resent his prodding. Selfishly, I thought, "He doesn't care how tired I get. All he thinks about is how many exercises I've done." I even missed his sympathy. After so many months of being completely dependent, it was hard to realize that the time had come for me to leave my safe little cocoon of dependence on him and try to do more for myself.

It was during this time of recovery that our beloved Pastor Bob and his family were called to a church in Oregon. His encouragement and inspiration had been our mainstay during those bitter, frightening months. We were heartsick, knowing the empty place he would leave in our hearts, yet we were thankful that God had placed him in our lives at a time when we were most needy.

The ladies from the church continued to care for me until Mary Shell, our cousin, decided to quit her job and care for me daily. It was easier now, and she and Vince planned a rigorous schedule to help me walk again.

If we had tried to celebrate each new achievement, we would have celebrated daily, for once the regeneration of muscles and nerves began, progress became visible every day. Each evening Vince rushed home, anxious to try something new. When standing became easier, he began placing my hands on the handles of my wheelchair; then holding me upright we would slowly walk down the hallway. At first it was only a few shaky steps, but gradually I walked a little farther each day. Oh, the excitement when we made it all the way into the living room!

When walking behind the wheelchair became easier, Vince brought home another surprise: a walker. With him still holding me up, we practiced. It was slower than the wheelchair, which made it easier for me to handle. Constant practice made the muscles stronger, and I became more confident. Soon I could take steps without Vince holding me up.

With added activity, my lungs began to clear up. It was a happy day when I was finally able to have the tracheotomy removed. Once the hole in my neck was closed, I was able to speak much more easily. However, it was some time before I felt confident enough to speak very much. It had been so long that carrying on a conversation was difficult in the beginning. That too soon changed!

The day finally came when I was left home alone for a few hours at a time. At first, being alone frightened me. I was still shaky and often fell when I tried to walk with the walker. My neighbor, Mary Carman, kept close watch on me when I was alone, giving me courage and support.

The lack of coordination caused many mishaps. As I related them to the family in the evenings, we made light of them, realizing that it was healthier to laugh at my accidents than to cry. I did a lot of both.

One morning, feeling adventurous, I decided to use my walker and cross the street. I wanted to surprise Mary before she came to check on me. Part way across the street my knees buckled and I fell. Frightened and hurt, I looked around. No one was in sight to help me. I was still unable to call out and could not get up by myself. After much effort I managed to crawl back across the street. The pavement dug into my knees. Dragging my walker behind me, I finally managed to get back home alone. However, instead of becoming discouraged, I felt triumphant and more determined than ever to succeed. Though I was bloodied and sore, the street had been a testing ground, and I had passed the test, not because I crossed, but because I conquered my own problem. I knew I might fall again, as I had many times before, but I would survive. I would never yield to failure.

Chapter 14
Job's Comforters

Again it was spring. A year had gone by since Vince and I stood outside enjoying the warm morning sun and admiring the spring flowers—the day our world turned upside down!

This year the daffodils were more beautiful than ever, the smell of spring sweeter, the sky more blue, the breeze balmier. Winter was over. New life was evident everywhere, especially the new life that was springing up in us.

It was hard to believe how far I had come from total paralysis. The road to recovery had been long and full of heartache and pain, of broken dreams and tormented minds. However, the journey was not over. In spite of the tremendous improvement, I was still affected by weakness and pain. Occasionally I cried out to God in confusion and frustration. Although God had not yet removed the disease, He continued giving strength to endure and faith to continue the struggle.

Spring gave way to summer, and our family looked forward to our first time away since our nightmare had begun. We set out for Colorado for a family reunion.

I was determined to walk without my walker on this trip. Vince and the boys helped me regain self-assurance as I struggled through those first faltering steps. Constant urging with love and enthusiasm bolstered my confidence as I finally stepped out alone. The joy of a baby's first steps could not compare to our joy and excitement as I took those first shaky steps, leaving the walker behind.

Our trip held an air of more than casual excitement. I was

81

like a bird set free, like a kite in the wind. We traveled toward our destination with carefree anticipation.

The reunion was held at a church camp in the mountains of Colorado, a perfect setting for such a special occasion. Being with the family again was wonderful.

While at the reunion, I was utterly surprised when several carloads of people came to the camp and began asking for me.

"Who are all these people?" I asked Vince, who was standing beside me. "And why are they asking for me?"

I stepped out, "I'm Dorothy Shell. Can I help you?" I said to the lady that appeared to be in charge.

"We can't believe it's really you," they all said excitedly as they began shaking my hand and hugging me.

"We're so pleased to see that you are able to walk and talk. We've been praying for you for a year now," the spokeslady said. "Last year at this time a woman from your church moved to Colorado. She came to a seminar held each year in the Denver area. She was so concerned about you that she shared with us your heart-rending story. This resulted in several 'Dorothy Shell' prayer groups being started. It's so wonderful to have been a part of this miraculous answer to prayer!"

I felt overwhelmed with gratitude for such concern from people I had never met. They began to relate stories of miraculous healings, conversions, and the restoration of marriages as a result of their prayer groups. I had come to Colorado for a family reunion. As I left I had been blessed, not only by the Shell family, but by the loving, caring family of God from many parts of the country.

After my return home, I began to reflect on the bleak days of paralysis. I could see God's hand leading me through the darkest hours. Even so, whenever pain returned, I again found myself complaining. I not only wanted God to take away the paralysis, but to free me from porphyria. This He had not done. Again I questioned, "Why had He restored strength to lifeless muscles and vibrations to silenced vocal chords, but had not removed the disease that caused all the trouble?" It didn't make sense, and Satan used this area of conflict in my life to cause doubt and confusion. Thus began a new type of testing.

Then came the accusers. Friends and acquaintances, sounding a lot like Job's comforters, told me, "Don't accept the pain. It's from Satan. All you need is faith. Exercise your faith, Dorothy, exercise your faith! God has healed you. All you need is to accept it!"

I was bombarded with advice and accusations. I had faith. How could I muster up more faith? The pain continued, and so did the accusers.

Hebrew 11:1 says, "What is faith? It is the confident assurance that something we want is going to happen. It is the certainty that what we hope for is waiting for us, even though we cannot see it up ahead." LB. Fervently I sought faith, only to discover that faith is a gift that comes from God. I could not muster it up on my own. I knew, too, that what I hoped for was still up ahead. I just did not know how far ahead.

During a time of intense pain and fatigue, I cried out, "Lord, what more can I do? If the accusers are right, show me. I can't go on trying to manufacture sufficient faith for healing. If complete healing is what you want for me now, show me. If acceptance is what I need, teach me how."

Seeking guidance from the Holy Spirit, I searched the Scriptures. Then it was that I found 2 Corinthians 12:7-10, where Paul talks about his "physical condition" (LB) or "thorn" in the flesh (NIV). He begged God three times to make him well. Each time God said, "No. But I am with you. . . . My power shows up best in weak people." Paul said, "Now I am glad to boast about how weak I am; . . . for when I am weak, then I am strong." LB.

The burden lifted. I felt a strange joy I could not explain as I came to accept my situation. I no longer needed to struggle for enough faith to believe. God was back in control. I would accept total healing gladly, but if I could be used the way I was for now, I wanted His will, not mine. The struggle was over. With release came a quiet peace, and even freedom from some of the pain.

The Scripture tells us that we should run with patience the race God has set before us, keeping our eyes only on Him. See Hebrews 12:1, 2.

My question now to the accusers was, "Must I be problem-free to be strong? If I have no weakness, how can I empathize with those who are weak?"

When you have struggled as hard as you can, for as long as you can, and have used up all your courage and all your strength, God will give you more so you can continue.

Chapter 15
Help Is in Sight

Vince sat at the big old desk in the basement struggling with the bills. There was never enough money to pay all of them. I had followed him downstairs this evening, just to be near him while he worked.

Our finances were a cause of deep concern to me. I was aware that I was the reason for most of the bills that lay on his desk. I had tried several jobs, only to find that my strength was too limited to carry through on them. Several times I pushed myself beyond the limits of my endurance and was forced to go back to bed for a period of time.

Vince appreciated my efforts, but he was more concerned that I stay well than that I provide extra income. However, I continued to look for something I could do to help. Something that would take limited time, yet be profitable. It was then that I was introduced to selling home decorations. Decorating was of great interest to me, so I decided to try. I could work when physically able, and rest when strength was limited. I really liked the products, and therefore I did well and was able to help pay some of the staggering medical bills.

My experience with Home Interiors was a rewarding one. As important as the friends and material gain were, most important was the sense of self-esteem I regained. One of the chief thoughts the company instilled in my mind was, "Be somebody. God didn't take time to make a nobody." I knew that with God's help, I could become whatever He wanted me to be.

I began to learn more and more about my disease, and in

time it became easier to ward off some of the attacks. Stress and fatigue were often the cause, so Vince and the boys watched for the signs and helped me to rest more and be less anxious. Knowing now that there was a reason for my illness and that it was not psychosomatic, it became easier to cope and occasionally control the attacks.

Today, several years later, it seems like yesterday that the boys were still in school. I can still hear them running up the walk, yelling, "Mom, I'm home." The house is quiet now. Those energetic kids are young men. In spite of the rocky teenage years and the traumatic effect my illness had on our sons, Alan, Rick, and Dennis grew to be fine young men. They have remained attentive and caring, finally leaving to make homes of their own. Vince and I miss the hustle and bustle of their active lives, but we have settled back, content for just the two of us to be together.

For a long time we found it increasingly difficult to talk about the past. Whenever the subject came up, Vince changed it. He pushed the painful memories back, as if trying to erase them completely from his mind.

Several years ago I began to realize that we both needed a healing of those memories. The opportunity came when we were invited to attend a Marriage Encounter weekend. What an outstanding experience that proved to be! It was here that we were able to reach out to each other and share the hurts and emotional pains produced by my long illness. We were drawn even closer as we began to sort out and understand the innermost feelings we had each felt during that devastating time in our lives.

As we were able to talk about the old hurts, we could see that it had been a growing experience. Our love for each other and for God was even stronger than before. The Lord had taken us past another milestone on our journey toward wholeness and healing.

One day the Lord began to show me that a new chapter in my life was about to be written. I began to have muscle spasms in my back, hips, and legs. The doctors tried everything they knew to relieve the pain, but instead of improvement, the muscles began to deteriorate. It became difficult for me to use my legs, and eventually my hands. Dr. Strouth became more and more concerned.

"If something isn't done soon, you'll be back in the wheelchair," he told me.

He also told me of a Dr. James P. Kushner in Salt Lake City, who was doing research on porphyria. "Possibly you could contact him," he said. "I am so sorry, but I have no answers for you."

I called Dr. Kushner, and he set a date for my first visit to Salt Lake City. Because I rarely looked ill, he, as many others before him, was skeptical that I even had porphyria. However, as usual the tests were positive, and more extensive testing was begun to determine the cause of the deterioration.

Dr. Jack Petijohn, a neurologist, was called in to do nerve conduction tests. The results showed extensive nerve damage and very little nerve conduction. This meant that the nerves were not communicating with the muscles. This was the cause of the deterioration.

Dr. Petijohn was amazed at my ability to use my legs and arms so well in light of the findings. He told me that when he first started the tests he thought the machine was not working properly. I used this opportunity to tell him that I knew whose strength I was operating on, and it was not my own.

Later Dr. Kushner explained to me that often in severe cases of porphyria, neurological damage was a problem. He also explained that he knew of nothing to stop the progress of deterioration, let alone reverse it.

Before coming to Salt Lake City, I had been told of a new drug called hematin that had been found to help patients who were having an acute attack of porphyria. I pleaded with Dr. Kushner to let me try the drug.

"But, Mrs. Shell," Dr. Kushner explained, "that drug has never been administered to reverse the damage already done."

However, I persisted, and Dr. Kushner finally agreed to call Dr. C. J. Watson in Minnesota, who discovered the drug. "Perhaps he will agree and let us try it in your case," he said.

After much consultation, the doctors decided to administer the drug. He cautioned me, however, that the outlook was not good. "We are not at all sure it will help," he said, "but since there seems to be nothing else we can do, as a last resort we will give it a try."

For a while after the doctor left that day, I was pretty discouraged. "What if this doesn't work?" The thought of being back in a wheelchair frightened me. For a while I cried. Yes, and I even began asking Why again. Gradually, though, I was able to leave it in God's hands. The burden lifted, the frustration left, and I began to get excited over the "medical breakthrough" that these injections could bring about.

Dr. Kushner did not share my optimistic enthusiasm.

The injections began. Five were to be given in a series. The first one went well, but some of the following ones caused a myriad of problems. The process was difficult, but anticipation of a possible recovery brought me through.

Following the fifth injection, I was again given the nerve conduction tests. Dr. Petijohn seemed surprised at my confidence that there would be a change for the better. He was more than surprised when his test showed some improvement! Though slight, the improvement was sufficient to encourage him and Dr. Watson to continue the injections at a later date.

As I left the hospital I felt an awareness that this could very well be a big step in the treatment of porphyria. I also believed that God was using me in a way I had never thought of before. Could this just possibly be one of the reasons the disease had not been completely taken away? This I could never know for sure, but I felt a peace that I did not yet understand.

I returned to Salt Lake City every four weeks for a period of time. Each time, five injections were given, and each time a slight improvement was noted. I regained full use of my hands and legs, and the pain eased. Even though good results were evident by the tests given, Dr. Kushner remained skeptical. I returned periodically for treatment and testing.

Two years passed as I enjoyed better health. Then the symptoms recurred. This time the pain and weakness in my legs and lower back became so severe that Dr. Kushner seriously thought of severing some of the nerves to relieve the pain. Instead, Vince and I decided to go to the University of Minnesota to see Dr. Joseph Bloomer, a specialist who had taken the place of Dr. Watson. While there, I was again subjected to extensive and painful nerve and motor muscle tests.

Again, as before, I was told the severity of my problem. And again the doctors could scarcely believe how much I was able to do in spite of the lack of conduction and motor response evident from the tests. In fact, they informed us that it was their opinion that I would be in a wheelchair soon. Doctor Bloomer encouraged us to begin to make plans for some type of nursing care at home.

With little hope or encouragement, Vince and I came home, wondering what the Lord had in mind for us now.

The weakness and pain remained for some time, and then gradually, just like it began, it diminished. Yes, occasionally I still have debilitating pain. However, I am now involved in a new experiment for porphyria. I read of a Dr. Richard Galbraith in New York who was looking for volunteers for testing in his study of porphyria. I called Dr. Galbraith at the Rockefeller University Hospital. Eventually I was accepted for the experiment.

A new type of hematin is now being tested called tin-heme. Each time I go I must spend four weeks at the hospital, and again it involves injections. I have had very little adverse reaction to the medication, and I am feeling better than I can ever remember.

I know not what lies ahead, whether good health will continue or not. I do know that God has used me and my illness in many more ways than I could ever have imagined. I have tried to use this malady as a steppingstone instead of a stumbling block. I pray that my part in these experiments may someday help others who are afflicted by this disease. I am not sure how I fit into God's plan, but I know whose I am, and I am willing to be used in whatever way He deems best.

Chapter 16
Looking Back

So many joys have been mine as God has helped me fight back after each trying episode of despair. The valleys have been many, but the mountaintop experiences have far outweighed the dark shadows of the valley below.

As I pass through the valleys, I am learning the wisdom of trusting God and not always asking, "Why did this happen to me?" I ask instead, "What can I do with it?" I am learning to be relaxed in His will, knowing He is still in control.

Looking back to that awesome night when life seemed to ebb from my body and I witnessed the love flowing from God's presence into my life, I realize how much more of life I have enjoyed and shared than was promised. Not only have I raised our sons, but beyond that I have seen them marry and now enjoy the love of several beautiful grandchildren. Now I can again hear those footsteps on the front walk, only this time I hear, "Grandma, we're here!" Again it's like the sound of music.

I've been able to help and encourage Vince as he established a print shop, a dream that seemed impossible because of so many roadblocks in our lives.

Vince and I make the most of my pain-free days. We are learning together the fullness of God's love manifested in our love for each other. After so many years of sickness and pain, we are learning how to glean the good from the bad as we reach a place of understanding and acceptance of God's hand upon our lives.

As we grow in acceptance, we realize that each person has

his own mountain to climb. I felt that my mountain had been higher and steeper than most, yet when I reached what I thought was the summit, I found that it was only a little knoll compared to the ones that reached to the skies above me.

The height of the peaks that I had surmounted had at first seemed absolutely impossible to climb. I was often completely discouraged with my ability to reach the summit. However, as we each ascend our own particular mountain, the way often seems steep and rocky. It would be easier to stop and turn back, but we know we must continue the climb. As we stop for a rest, we look up, hoping the summit is in view, only to see that it reaches even higher than we had expected. These are the times we get discouraged and feel we will never, but never, reach the top.

Often I became so intent on the climb that I failed to notice the beauty of the scenery around me. Now, I wonder, if we would stop and look back down to the valley below at the breathtaking beauty, might we gain a new perspective? Then when both soul and body are satisfied, we might be better able to scale the remainder of the mountain with renewed vigor.

My long illness has been my special mountain. I can and I will reach the top. I am still unsure of the distance I have left to travel, but I will come out on top where the sun shines and the whole world comes into view.

There are indeed times when I can rest from the climb. On one of these resting times I was privileged to again spend a few days by the beautiful Payette Lake in McCall, where Vince and I spent our honeymoon. As I sat by the lake I noticed how still the water was. It had become quiet and peaceful, looking like glass. The reflection of the boats resting quietly in the harbor made the whole world seem at peace. I observed a large sailboat completely at rest in the still waters. A breeze stirred, and as the wind gained a little strength, the sailboat began to move. The more troubled the waters became, the faster it sailed through the water. Once again, I felt as if the Lord was speaking to my soul.

"Rest while the waters are still, rest while I calm the sea, for the day is coming when I will again trouble the waters that you can move within My will."

I knew that no matter how alone I had felt or would feel in the days to come, He had been and would always be with me.

My course is set. Together the Lord and I have embarked on a new adventure into His will. No mountain is too high, no water too choppy. The beauty of God will shine through, and when all the mountains have been conquered and all the seas have been crossed, He will say, "Well done, my good and faithful servant, enter into the joy of your Lord." See Matthew 25:23.

By God's grace, and only by His grace, the journey will be successful, because I believe that a perfect God reigns over an imperfect world.